Praise for *Coherence* by Michael Fullan and Joanne Quinn

"Coherence is a book that demands action—it moves from the narrative of fixing one teacher at a time to asking about the coherence of the system (be it school, national, or world issues). Fullan and Quinn create an important narrative about direction, working together, deepening learning, and securing accountability. The book sparkles with examples of coherence in action; it makes no excuses for employing the wrong levers of change. This is the blueprint for a new vocabulary of education action; it shows where we need to go next, and is another example of Fullan at the top of his game."

John Hattie, Director
Melbourne Education Research Institute
and Author of *Visible Learning*

"I love this book—timely, practical collaborative action! In an era of overload, frustration, and fatigue, *Coherence* offers an extremely timely, necessary, and practical alternative to improving education. *Coherence* is essentially about the power, potential, and promise of people working collaboratively: the humanity and professional capacity of educators seeking to lead, learn, and teach to realize the persistent moral purpose of supporting all students to succeed. A hallmark of *Coherence* is that the principles and actions are grounded in practical examples from schools, districts, and entire education systems. We desperately need coherence; this book provides a vital framework for collective action!"

Carol Campbell, Associate Professor
Ontario Institute for Studies in Education
University of Toronto

"With the improvement of student learning at the center, *Coherence* assists educational leaders at every level to choose strategic drivers for change, learn collaboratively, and deliver results collectively. Fullan and Quinn nail the solution: building coherence is an ongoing process that focuses on quality implementation of a small number of powerful goals that improve student learning. The Coherence Framework pushes and supports all leaders to improve their practice in the service of students."

John Malloy, EdD, Assistant Deputy Minister
Leadership and Learning Environment Division
Ministry of Education

"School systems that struggle are often riddled with incoherence— mismatched strategies, competing cultures, and illogical initiatives. In their highly informative book, Fullan and Quinn clearly explain how coherence can solve the problem. Based on solid research and lessons drawn from effective practice, *Coherence* provides a comprehensive model to guide educators as they learn and lead their way to better schools."

Susan Moore Johnson, Jerome T. Murphy Research Professor
Harvard Graduate School of Education

"*Coherence* is a must-read for educators and politicians who are ready to talk the walk and take action with the 'right drivers.' As a site and district leader I learned from reformers and researchers alike, but I struggled to operationalize what I had learned to benefit the adults and students I served. In *Coherence,* Fullan and Quinn clearly articulate a plan for operationalizing the 'right drivers' throughout the system—school site, district, county, state, and nation."

Wes Smith, Executive Director
Association of California School Administrators

"Michael Fullan and Joanne Quinn have hit it out of the park in their new book *Coherence*. This book is an excellent resource for any school or school system that is committed to continuous improvement. *Coherence* is a practical, powerful action guide for schools and school systems to use as they work collaboratively to close the achievement gap that exists in our schools. This book should be the required reading for all school administrators and elected officials."

Chris Steinhauser, Superintendent
Long Beach Unified School District, California

Coherence

Coherence

*The Right Drivers in Action
for Schools, Districts, and Systems*

. . . .

Michael Fullan

Joanne Quinn

. . . .

A Joint Publication of

A SAGE Company

FOR INFORMATION:

Corwin

A SAGE Company

2455 Teller Road

Thousand Oaks, California 91320

(800) 233-9936

www.corwin.com

SAGE Publications Ltd.

1 Oliver's Yard

55 City Road

London EC1Y 1SP

United Kingdom

SAGE Publications India Pvt. Ltd.

B 1/I 1 Mohan Cooperative Industrial Area

Mathura Road, New Delhi 110 044

India

SAGE Publications Asia-Pacific Pte. Ltd.

3 Church Street

#10-04 Samsung Hub

Singapore 049483

Graphics by Taryn Hauritz.

Printed in the United States of America

ISBN 978-1-4833-6495-7

This book is printed on acid-free paper.

Executive Editor: Arnis Burvikovs

Senior Associate Editor: Desirée A. Bartlett

Editorial Assistant: Andrew Olson

Production Editor: Melanie Birdsall

Copy Editor: Megan Markanich

Typesetter: C&M Digitals (P) Ltd.

Proofreader: Christine Dahlin

Indexer: Karen Wiley

Cover Designer: Anupama Krishnan

Marketing Manager: Amy Vader

Certified Chain of Custody
SUSTAINABLE FORESTRY INITIATIVE
Promoting Sustainable Forestry
www.sfiprogram.org
SFI-01268

SFI label applies to text stock

16 17 18 19 10 9 8 7 6 5

Contents

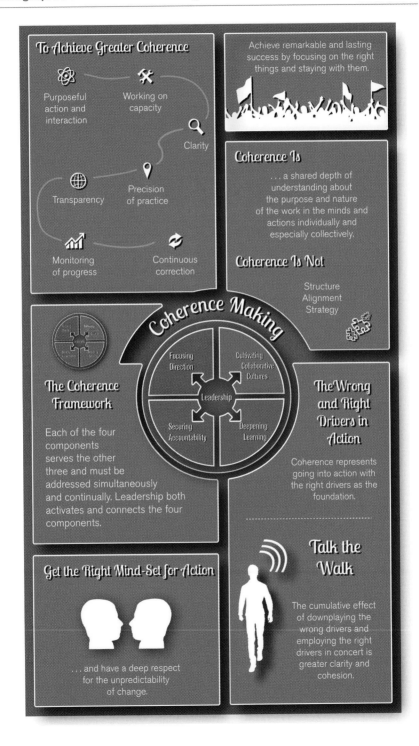

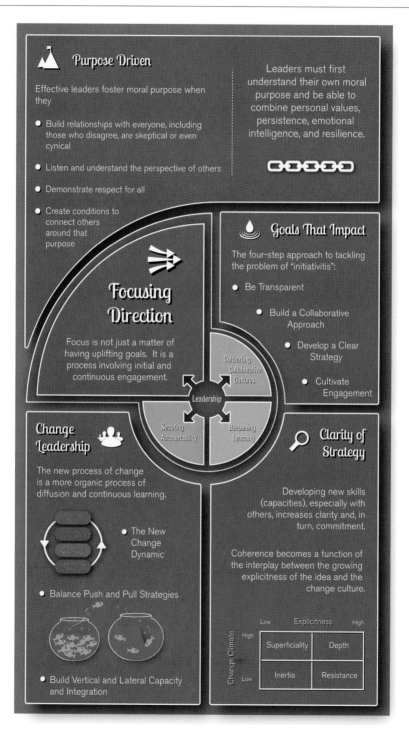

Purpose Driven

Effective leaders foster moral purpose when they

- Build relationships with everyone, including those who disagree, are skeptical or even cynical

- Listen and understand the perspective of others

- Demonstrate respect for all

- Create conditions to connect others around that purpose

Leaders must first understand their own moral purpose and be able to combine personal values, persistence, emotional intelligence, and resilience.

Focusing Direction

Focus is not just a matter of having uplifting goals. It is a process involving initial and continuous engagement.

Goals That Impact

The four-step approach to tackling the problem of "initiativitis":

- Be Transparent

- Build a Collaborative Approach

- Develop a Clear Strategy

- Cultivate Engagement

Cultivating Collaborative Cultures

Leadership

Securing Accountability

Deepening Learning

Change Leadership

The new process of change is a more organic process of diffusion and continuous learning.

- The New Change Dynamic

- Balance Push and Pull Strategies

- Build Vertical and Lateral Capacity and Integration

Clarity of Strategy

Developing new skills (capacities), especially with others, increases clarity and, in turn, commitment.

Coherence becomes a function of the interplay between the growing explicitness of the idea and the change culture.

	Low Explicitness High	
High	Superficiality	Depth
Low	Inertia	Resistance

Change Climate

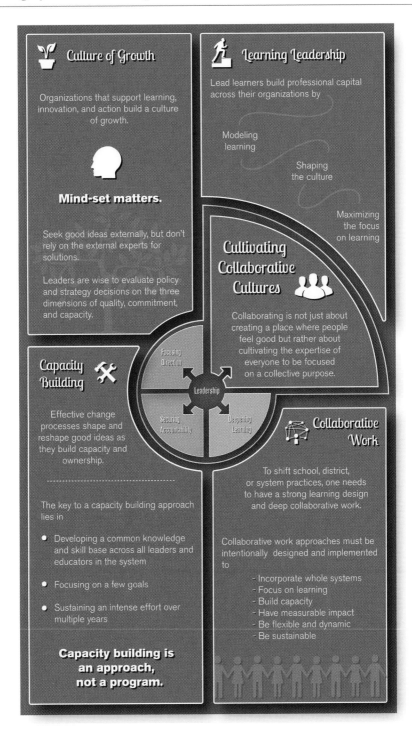

Culture of Growth

Organizations that support learning, innovation, and action build a culture of growth.

Mind-set matters.

Seek good ideas externally, but don't rely on the external experts for solutions.

Leaders are wise to evaluate policy and strategy decisions on the three dimensions of quality, commitment, and capacity.

Learning Leadership

Lead learners build professional capital across their organizations by

Modeling learning

Shaping the culture

Maximizing the focus on learning

Cultivating Collaborative Cultures

Collaborating is not just about creating a place where people feel good but rather about cultivating the expertise of everyone to be focused on a collective purpose.

Focusing Direction

Leadership

Securing Accountability

Deepening Learning

Capacity Building

Effective change processes shape and reshape good ideas as they build capacity and ownership.

The key to a capacity building approach lies in

- Developing a common knowledge and skill base across all leaders and educators in the system

- Focusing on a few goals

- Sustaining an intense effort over multiple years

Capacity building is an approach, not a program.

Collaborative Work

To shift school, district, or system practices, one needs to have a strong learning design and deep collaborative work.

Collaborative work approaches must be intentionally designed and implemented to

- Incorporate whole systems
- Focus on learning
- Build capacity
- Have measurable impact
- Be flexible and dynamic
- Be sustainable

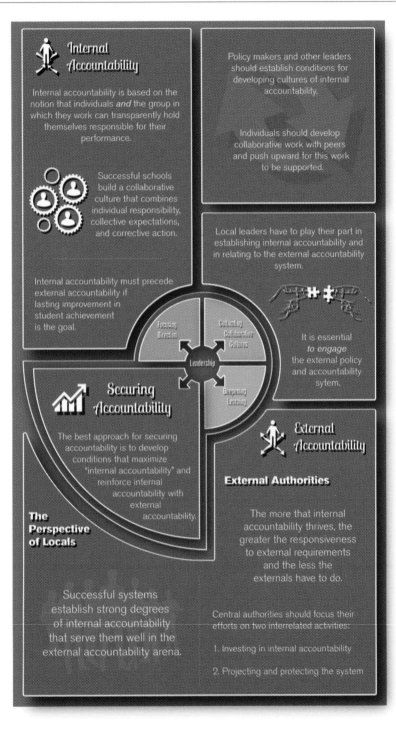

Internal Accountability

Internal accountability is based on the notion that individuals *and* the group in which they work can transparently hold themselves responsible for their performance.

Successful schools build a collaborative culture that combines individual responsibility, collective expectations, and corrective action.

Internal accountability must precede external accountability if lasting improvement in student achievement is the goal.

Policy makers and other leaders should establish conditions for developing cultures of internal accountability.

Individuals should develop collaborative work with peers and push upward for this work to be supported.

Local leaders have to play their part in establishing internal accountability and in relating to the external accountability system.

It is essential *to engage* the external policy and accountability sytem.

Focusing Direction

Cultivating Collaborative Cultures

Leadership

Deepening Learning

Securing Accountability

The best approach for securing accountability is to develop conditions that maximize "internal accountability" and reinforce internal accountability with external accountability.

The Perspective of Locals

Successful systems establish strong degrees of internal accountability that serve them well in the external accountability arena.

External Accountability

External Authorities

The more that internal accountability thrives, the greater the responsiveness to external requirements and the less the externals have to do.

Central authorities should focus their efforts on two interrelated activities:

1. Investing in internal accountability

2. Projecting and protecting the system

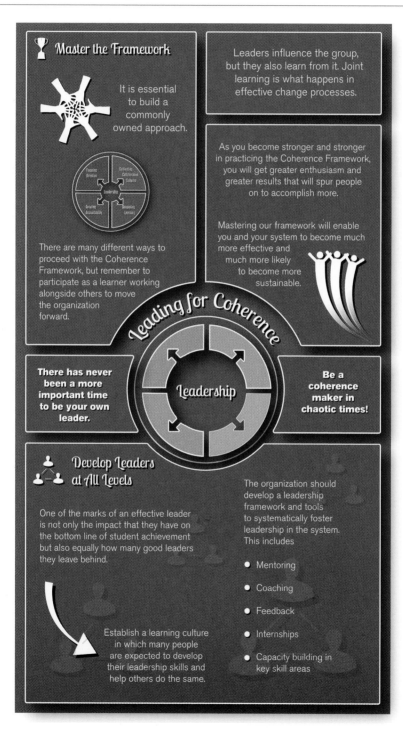

Master the Framework

It is essential to build a commonly owned approach.

There are many different ways to proceed with the Coherence Framework, but remember to participate as a learner working alongside others to move the organization forward.

Leaders influence the group, but they also learn from it. Joint learning is what happens in effective change processes.

As you become stronger and stronger in practicing the Coherence Framework, you will get greater enthusiasm and greater results that will spur people on to accomplish more.

Mastering our framework will enable you and your system to become much more effective and much more likely to become more sustainable.

There has never been a more important time to be your own leader.

Leading for Coherence

Leadership

Be a coherence maker in chaotic times!

Develop Leaders at All Levels

One of the marks of an effective leader is not only the impact that they have on the bottom line of student achievement but also equally how many good leaders they leave behind.

Establish a learning culture in which many people are expected to develop their leadership skills and help others do the same.

The organization should develop a leadership framework and tools to systematically foster leadership in the system. This includes

- Mentoring
- Coaching
- Feedback
- Internships
- Capacity building in key skill areas

Authors' Note

The Time Is Now!

How do you turn overload and fragmentation into focus and coherence? This is what this book is about.

We have been involved in developing coherence for student learning in districts and systems (provinces/states) since 1988. We have helped practitioners do this, but more than that, they have helped us understand the details. This work—bringing about system change within reasonably short timelines—has become increasingly clear. It is difficult to do but not overwhelming. And once you get the knack of it, the process of change moves more quickly and deeply (see Fullan, in press).

Part of the subtitle of the book is "right drivers in action." In 2011, one of us, Fullan, wrote a policy paper titled "Choosing the Wrong Drivers for Whole System Reform" (2011a). The wrong drivers were external accountability, individualism, technology, and ad hoc policies. The corresponding right drivers were capacity building with a focus on results, collaboration, pedagogy, and systemness (coordinated policies).

The wrong drivers paper immediately hit a responsive chord especially at the middle (district and regions) and school levels. Many leaders embraced the distinction and were quick to denounce the wrong driver tendencies of policy makers. But our "drivers paper" was not a plan of action (if you like, it was better at describing what not to do than it was at figuring out what actually to do). Thus, *Coherence* represents going into action with the right drivers as the foundation.

The Coherence Framework has four components: focusing direction, cultivating collaborative cultures, deepening learning, and securing accountability. Separate chapters delve deeply into each of the components. We will also show how the four elements intersect to form a dynamic whole and how leadership at all levels is essential for integrating the core ideas. The action framework we have developed aligns to the original four right drivers as follows:

Original Right Drivers	Right Drivers in Action
Systemness	Focusing Direction
Collaboration	Cultivating Collaborative Cultures
Pedagogy	Deepening Learning
Capacity Building for Results	Securing Accountability

- *Focusing direction* is systemness (the need to integrate what the system is doing).
- *Cultivating collaborative cultures* oversees individualism by producing strong groups and strong individuals.
- *Deepening learning,* which is founded on new pedagogical partnerships, is the driver for better outcomes using technology as the accelerator.
- Capacity for results is based on developing skills and competencies within the group that, in turn, serves as a basis for being self-responsible and accountable to the outside. The road to *securing accountability* is through developing capacity within the group that, in turn, interfaces with the external accountability system.

At the center of the framework is leadership. Leaders must find the right combination of these four components to meet the varying needs of their context. One last clarifying point is this: We don't have capacity building as a separate component in the Coherence Framework because particular capacities are contained and necessary within each of the four components. Leadership, thus, infuses capacity building into all levels and work of the system as it combines the four components.

The audience for this book includes leaders at all levels of the education system—school and community, district and region, and state level. For those at the school and district/regional levels, you can take action using the Coherence Framework directly. State-level people have a double agenda: use the framework in your own actions but also create the infrastructure of policy, budget, and partnerships at the middle and local levels for "whole system improvement" to flourish. Our approach is a win-win proposition, but it has to be deliberately fostered by many leaders working individually and collectively.

The term *simplexity* captures what we do. We take a complicated matter, identify the smallest number of key factors or domains (typically four to six), and work together with practitioners to become clear about and to master the factors in actions. The simple part is the small number of key domains; the complex part is making the ideas gel or cohere with all participants, given the politics, pressures, and personalities involved. The good news is that it works. It is doable and as such is catching on. Wallowing in confusion is not all that enjoyable. Our alternative is much more satisfying. Most people would rather be challenged by change and helped to progress than be mired in frustration. Best of all, this work tackles "whole systems" and uses the group to change the group. People know they are engaged in something beyond their narrow role. It is human nature to rise to a larger call *if* the problems are serious enough and *if* there is a way forward where they can play a role with others. Coherence making is the pathway that does this.

You will see in this book how Garden Grove Unified School District overcame the challenge of high poverty, with over 80 percent English-language learners (ELLs) to become one of the highest-performing districts in the state of California. You will witness how the province of Ontario took a stagnant school system of 5,000 schools and 72 districts and transformed it into one of the highest-performing systems in the world. You will find out how a highly diverse urban school district, York Region District School Board, with some 200 schools declared literacy—the ability of children to read by the end of grade 1 and to read well by grade 3—priority number one and then proceeded to make it a reality in less than a decade. And you will see how principal James Bond (no, not *that* James Bond) and his teachers at Park Manor Senior Public School formed a strong base of pedagogy and then used digital to accelerate learning, moving to high proficiency in writing from 42 percent of the students to 83 percent achieving at those levels.

All of these systems, and others we cite, used "coherence making strategies" as the route to success. They focused direction, employed collaborative capacity building, went deep in pedagogy, and secured internal group-based accountability across the whole system. The researcher John Hattie (2015) has added further confirmation to our conclusions in his report *What Works Best in Education: The Politics of Collaborative Expertise*. His conclusion represents a powerful endorsement of our findings: "the greatest influence on student progression in learning is having highly expert, inspired and passionate teachers and school leaders working together to maximize the effect of their teaching on all students in their care" (p. 2).

Our book is a story of how regular school systems can achieve remarkable and lasting success by focusing on the right things and staying with them. For the first time, these strategies are accessible to all. Our intent in this book is to make coherence making an understandable and valuable resource for leaders who want to make a lasting difference.

1

Coherence Making

It is time to make good on the promise of public education. Our children need it, the public is demanding it, and indeed the world needs it to survive and thrive. Public education is humankind's future—for better or worse. For the first time, we have the knowledge and expertise to deliver. What we need is consistency of purpose, policy, and practice. Structure and strategy are not enough. The solution requires the individual and collective ability to build shared meaning, capacity, and commitment to action. When large numbers of people have a deeply understood sense of what needs to be done—and see their part in achieving that purpose—coherence emerges and powerful things happen.

In this chapter, we define what coherence is and is not, describe the "wrong and right drivers," and provide the Coherence Framework that forms the basis of the solution and the chapters in this book.

What Coherence Is and Is Not

Merriam-Webster defines *coherence* as the "integration of diverse elements, relationships, or values." Images of coherence have to do with making sense, sticking together, and connecting. Note that these elements relate to what people on the ground, so to speak, find coherent and meaningful. This gives us a hint as to what coherence is not. It is not structure. It is not alignment (although that can help) as when those in charge can explain how things fit (really, how things, *should fit* from their perspective). It is not strategy.

Coherence pertains to people individually and especially collectively. To cut to the chase, coherence consists of the shared depth of understanding about the purpose and nature of the work. Coherence, then, is what is in the minds and actions of people individually and especially collectively. We can see instantly why coherence is so difficult to accomplish under conditions of overload, fragmentation, and policy churn. Yet it can be done. There is only one way to achieve greater coherence, and that is through purposeful action and interaction, working on capacity, clarity, precision of practice, transparency, monitoring of progress, and continuous correction. All of this requires the right mixture of "pressure and support": the press for progress within supportive and focused cultures.

As critical masses of people engaged in coherence making evolve, it becomes more powerful, almost self-sustaining. In Ontario, where we have developed many of these ideas over the past 15 years, we stumbled on an indirect indicator of sustained coherence when scores of visitors came on study visits to see what our schools, districts, and Ministry of Education (state department) were doing in practice. They visited different schools; talked to teachers, principals, and students; met with district leaders; and had discussions with policy makers and those in the ministry who were in charge of the effort. There was a single thing that amazed the visitors almost universally. They said that when they asked various people about the main priorities, the strategies in action, progress, results, next steps, and so on, what they got was consistency and specificity across schools and across levels (see Fullan & Rincón-Gallardo, in press, for an analysis of the Ontario strategy). We have come to call this phenomenon the ability for those in the system to "talk the walk." We all know about "walk the talk," a good quality but not sufficient by itself. When people can talk the walk, you know that it is the real McCoy. When people can explain themselves specifically, they become clearer; when they can explain the ideas and actions to each other, they become mutually influential. When large numbers of people come to do this over time they socialize newcomers, and the whole thing becomes sustainable. Coherence making and its key components that we establish in this book are about this deep specificity and clarity of action.

One other crucial point about coherence is this: you never arrive once and for all, nor should you want to. There are always new developments so that you need to be plugged into innovations and the wider knowledge arena (without becoming an innovation junkie), there are always newcomers and change in leadership, and the perfect group does not last forever (thankfully nor does the terrible group). Coherence making in other words is a continuous process of making and remaking meaning in your own mind and in your culture. Our framework shows you how to do this.

The Wrong and Right Drivers in Action

I (Fullan) wrote a policy paper five years ago called "Choosing the Wrong Drivers for Whole System Reform" (Fullan, 2011a). The wrong drivers are punitive accountability, individualistic strategies, technology, and ad hoc policies. It is not that these factors should never be included but rather that we should not *lead* with them. Instead, I suggested that there is a set of right drivers that are effective: capacity building, collaboration, pedagogy, and systemness (coordinated policies).

Coherence provides the remedy to the wrong driver approach. We have renamed the right drivers into an action framework consisting of four main components: *focusing direction, cultivating collaborative cultures, deepening learning,* and *securing accountability.*

Our wrong driver analysis showed how politicians were making matters worse by imposing solutions that were crude and demotivating for the very people who have to help lead the solution—teachers and administrators. In the United States, various forms of these wrong drivers have been intensively in place since 2001, starting with No Child Left Behind and moving to Race to the Top and its associated components such as high-stakes teacher evaluation. Because they take a structural—and indeed negative—approach to change, they have no chance of generating coherence. They have, in other words, no chance of working.

You might ask why politicians endorse solutions that don't work. The answer is not complicated: because they can legislate them; because they are in a hurry; because the remedies can be made to appeal superficially to the public; because (and unkindly on our part) some of them really don't care about the *public* education system, preferring that education be taken over by the private sector; and (more kindly) because they do not know what else to do.

Wherever we go in the world and ask educators what issues they are facing, at the top of the list is confusion and overload, variously expressed as the following:

- Initiative fatigue
- Ad hoc projects
- Arbitrary top-down policies
- Compliance-oriented bureaucratization
- Silos and fiefdoms everywhere
- Confusion
- Distrust and demoralization

The more that system leaders try to correct the problem, the worse it gets. At the top of the list is punitive accountability. Daniel Pink (2009) has shown conclusively that this "carrots and sticks" approach works at best for only the most mechanical tasks, not for anything that requires ingenuity and commitment. You don't get coherence by imposing diktats.

Decision makers also have turned their attention to individualistic strategies—let's attract and reward better teachers, better school principals, and so on. Good individuals are important, but cultures are more so. As we will see if you want to change a group, an organization, or a system, you actually have to focus on the culture as well as the individuals within it. The culture will eat up individuals faster than you can produce them—so we focus on culture and on individuals simultaneously.

To make matters worse, the first two wrong drivers are often used in tandem. Focus on individuals and employ punitive accountability. These dual forces make matters worse. Once you face tasks where judgment is required, people do not respond to monetary rewards or threat of punishment. In challenging situations, people are motivated primarily by intrinsic factors: having a sense of purpose, solving difficult problems, and working with peers on issues that are of critical importance to the group. Attempting to entice individuals through extrinsic rewards and sanctions demotivates most people.

The third wrong driver that needs to be recast is technology. We ourselves are increasingly committed to integrating digital into our whole system change strategies (Fullan, 2013c), but this is in the face of the history of technology as a solution that can be summed up in one word—*acquisition.*

The tacit assumption is that if you want to be progressive, buy more digital devices. If you want to add to the confusion, layer on a bunch of technology.

The fourth and final bad driver is ad hoc policies. Politicians try to solve problems one at a time or simultaneously through separate initiatives. Let's call this the silo problem. One part addresses teachers, another administrators, still another technology, curriculum, standards, and so on. Implementers receive them exactly as delivered—a stream, a torrent, or a trickle—arriving as waves of segmented remedies. "Initiativitis" is enough to give change a bad name.

Note that the wrong drivers operate perversely. Each one is ineffective enough on its own, but they usually appear together like amateur actors in a bad movie! The result is that people are always off balance. Even those with the greatest motivation end up getting discouraged.

This book is about "what else to do." We know this because we work closely with education systems around the world, partnering with them to figure out and implement what works. The work is characterized by five things:

1. It is all about doing, working from practice to theory, and getting better by doing more with added knowledge.

2. It is about whole systems—all the schools and all the students in the district, state, province, and country.

3. It zeroes in on precise pedagogy—what works in promoting engaging learning for students and teachers alike.

4. It identifies and establishes the conditions, the cultures if you like, at the school, region, and broad infrastructure levels that push for and support deep implementation.

5. It always determines impact on learners and those who relate to them.

Through working with large numbers of people on this agenda, we have identified four so-called right drivers for whole system change: capacity building, collaboration, pedagogy, and systemness. These elements form the basis of our action strategy for whole system improvement that we spell out later as the Coherence Framework.

Capacity building refers to the skills, competencies, and knowledge that individuals and groups need in order to be effective at accomplishing the goals at hand. We generally think of them in two bins: the pedagogical bin (expert teaching and learning) and the change bin (expert leadership for change). We have developed and integrated both of these capacities on the ground in partnership with practitioners especially over the past decade.

The next driver, collaboration, involves the development of social capital. Social capital is the quality of the group, or as we say, if you want to change the group, use the group to change the group. A succinct example comes from the work of business professor Carrie Leana (2011) from the University of Pittsburgh. Leana typically measures three things in schools: human capital (the qualifications of individuals), social capital (with questions to teachers like "to what extent do you and other teachers in the school work in a collaborative focused way to improve the learning of all students in the school?"), and progress in math achievement from September to June. While she finds that some teachers with higher human capital get good results, the schools with higher social capital got the best overall math gains. Leana also found that many teachers with lower human capital who happened to be working in schools with high social capital also did better at increasing math achievement. Social capital is more powerful than human capital, and they function virtuously by feeding on each other (see also Hargreaves & Fullan, 2012).

Third, if you mix in good pedagogy as the driver (versus technology) as part of the content of capacity building and social capital exchanges, you get a triple benefit. The synergy is powerful. Good pedagogy is what teachers like to do every day. It is close to their hearts and minds, individually and collectively. *Then* you can integrate digital that, under these conditions, becomes an amazing accelerator and deepener of learning.

Fourth, figuring out how to achieve systemness by making the policy framework more cohesive is difficult and deceptive. As we have said, you can't just align the policies on paper. This theoretical or delivered alignment has little to do with how people in the field experience it. Coherence making, in other words, has to be achieved at the receiving end, not the delivery end. We will offer a solution in subsequent chapters, but essentially, it involves a combination of a small number of ambitious goals being relentlessly pursued, being vigilant about reducing distractors, helping with professional capacity building, using student and other data transparently for developmental purposes, building in strategies for implementers to learn from each other on an ongoing basis, and marking progress with lots of feedback and supportive intervention.

The cumulative effect of downplaying the wrong drivers and employing the right drivers in concert is greater clarity and cohesion. The right drivers on the move mean two things: political ascendancy and concrete examples on the ground. In this shift to more effective system solutions, politicians begin to embrace the drivers and enact them in legislation and strategic action. Ontario was the first. The drivers are firmly embedded in the politics and practices of the sector from top to bottom and laterally across the system (Fullan & Rincón-Gallardo, in press). Another jurisdiction that has politically taken up the right drivers is the state of California—again from top to bottom and sideways. The governor, Jerry Brown, has enacted legislation to decentralize funding and accountability actions; the state board and the California Department of Education (CDE) are repositioning themselves to support the new direction; the unions, the California Teachers Association, and the American Federation of Teachers are becoming more and more involved in the professional capital agenda; the statewide administrator association (Association of California School Administrators [ACSA]), with its 1,009 school districts and 17,000 members, has explicitly aligned itself to the right driver agenda, as are the county offices; many districts and especially clusters of districts are becoming engaged, from the very large California Office of Reform in Education (CORE) with its 10 districts, to the small consortia of three districts that we lead, and numerous other district clusters that are forming; and many statewide interest groups and associations support the new direction (for an overview of the California situation, see *California's Golden Opportunity: A Status Note* [Fullan, 2014a]). In short—and we are still speaking politically—some states are showing strong interest in moving toward the right driver agenda. And, of course, if California embeds more of these ideas and starts getting significant results, it could have a cascading effect across the country. Beyond all of this, scores of individual school districts across North America are incorporating the elements of right drivers as they blunt the presence of wrong drivers.

The second way that right drivers are on the move involves the greater specification and development of what the strategy looks like in practice. The original formulation was only a framework, not a plan. We have been working with many partners at the school, district, and state levels to spell out in more detail how small and very large systems can find and sustain focus.

Coherence is our attempt to spell out the solution that anyone can master with focus and persistence. We offer core insights and a simple but powerful framework for action. We see our book as helping schools and districts and systems achieve greater cohesion. We also direct our messages and ideas to provinces, states, and countries where system cohesion can pay off for everyone—literally benefiting the society as a whole.

There has to be an abiding focus and set of integrating forces at play. The initial right drivers set these forces in motion, and our developed version of the drivers in action take us to the next stage. One method we use to get at the most practical, powerful, cohesive ideas is to work with practitioners who have done it and to ask them what they were thinking and how they went about it. Two of these people are Laura Schwalm, who was superintendent from 2000 to 2013, and her successor, Gabriela Mafi, of Garden Grove Unified School District in the Anaheim area. Garden Grove is high-poverty and diverse (mostly Latinos and Vietnamese, with some 85 percent on free lunch) and has about 80 schools. When Schwalm began her stint, the district was well below the state average on all measures of performance. Steadily thereafter, and to the present, they have moved well above the state average (for a third-party research study, see Knudson, 2013). Here is what Schwalm (personal communication, July 2014) highlights about the journey:

> You need to be preoccupied with focus: a state or condition permitting clear perception or understanding; to direct your attention or effort to something specific; a main purpose or interest; direction. With so many issues that feel urgent, the necessity to focus is often overwhelmed by the number and magnitude of the problems faced by the system leader. You need "one main thing" or central

improvement strategy that consists of the leaders' nonnegotiable view of what, over time, will have the greatest impact on improving the systems performance for children. As superintendent of GGUSD [Garden Grove Unified School District], my big circle was "increasing the capacity of the adults in the system to support improved student outcomes." Within that circle, I prioritized building teacher capacity by focusing on improved pedagogy and building principal capacity to support teacher growth. While that was my first priority, the focus also included building capacity of classified employees and building the capacity of parents to support what teachers were asking of students as well as to push on us. Each of these had multiple entry points, which evolved over the years, and as we made strides in each we continued to refine the work.

Gabriela Mafi is carrying on and deepening the work at Garden Grove. Schwalm now works with us more widely in California in maximizing what we call "leadership from the middle" (LFTM). LFTM is based on the assumption that the center (the government) cannot effectively run large complex systems and that local school autonomy, if left on its own, will never add up. Hargreaves and Braun (2012) first identified LFTM as a powerful strategy—hence, the notion that clusters of districts working and learning together on specific solutions and working on coherence, really, is the way to go. There are a growing number of overlapping clusters of districts (over 50 clusters in our last count) working in such fashion. With 1,009 districts, greater coherence through the middle can be a powerful force for coherence statewide. The idea is that these clusters become better partners upward to the state and within their own communities through greater focus and capacity.

Speaking of the whole state, we also asked Davis Campbell, one of our close colleagues and partners in this work, why he thought the right drivers was the way to go. Campbell has seen it all over the past four decades in California. Campbell is a former deputy superintendent of the CDE (where in our language he was in charge of implementing the wrong drivers) and is currently on the board of the Stuart Foundation (one of the main funders of the right drivers work in the state) and on the faculty at UC Davis, where he has helped develop a superintendent leadership program. Here is what he said:

> California has always been known as having a strong top-down education governance system. But this system has also, in recent years, been characterized as very dysfunctional with shifting power centers at the state level. All of this has led to a high level of stress between the state educational agency and school districts.
>
> For the state education agency in California to be truly effective, there needs to be a conscious shift in both the mind-set of the staff and the basic culture of the organization. Historically, the Department of Education has operated on the assumption that mandating statewide reforms could solve problems in public education and that the state's job was to police districts to ensure that the state requirements, which define those programs or reforms, were met. This created a basic compliance mind-set and organizational culture in the department. It also created a perception that the people in Sacramento knew better than the professionals in the districts. The state has focused on inputs to districts rather than helping them improve their outputs to children.
>
> School districts, however, need something very different. They need professional leadership from the state that is informed by deep thinking about strategies that help districts build capacity to undergo systems change. The districts need the state to understand that major reforms such as the Local Control Funding Formula will have limited impact on their own unless they are utilized as tools to open up the system.
>
> The state projects a top-down image, districts want a resource, and a partner not a parent. What districts don't need are more rules and regulations. What they need and want is a state agency whose primary goal and mission, their internal compass so to speak, is to find ways to connect them with high-performing professionals and systems in a collaborative and mutually reinforcing way. The state needs to help find ways to empower successful professionals, in both teaching and administration, and provide them the opportunity to influence their colleagues in a comprehensive, sustained way.

School districts need the state to understand accountability as a strengthening process not a punitive exercise designed to punish for lack of performance according to state process requirements. (D. Campbell, personal communication, 2014; see also Fullan, 2014b; Michael Fullan Enterprises & California Forward, 2015, for status reports on what we refer to as "California's Golden Opportunity")

We are seeing a growing interest in policy and practice in embracing the right drivers framework from countries, states, provinces, districts, and schools. More and more educators are saying to us "we agree with this direction, but *how* do we do it?" This book represents where we are in this "how" quest. Arising from our work with districts and states, we have developed a model—the Coherence Framework—that will guide the rest of the chapters.

··
The Coherence Framework
··

What we need is a framework that can guide action and that is comprehensive but not unwieldy—something that works and that can be mastered by any leader or group that puts in the time to learn how the main elements fit in their own situation. This is the framework we have developed in working with the Schwalms and Campbells of the world and is depicted in Figure 1.1.

Our goal is to help others—scores of others—become immersed in work that develops focus and coherence across complex systems. We set out to show clearly that there is "something else" other than the constellation of wrong policy drivers and that this alternative works because it stimulates and motivates hordes of system members to rise to the occasion and experience the satisfaction of coherence amidst an otherwise messy world.

The four components of Figure 1.1 work together. It is important to understand the inner workings of each component as we do in successive chapters, but the big message is that they go together and must be addressed simultaneously and continually from day one. Think of each of the four components, the right drivers in action, as serving the other three. The total interaction effects are linked through leadership and are powerful.

Figure 1.1 The Coherence Framework

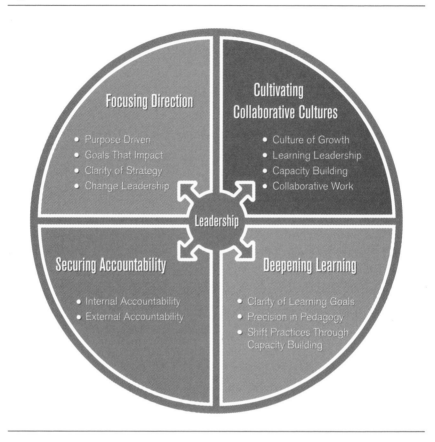

Focusing direction operationalizes the systemness dynamic vis-à-vis ad hoc policies. This component plays an overriding role because the moral imperative and directional vision are crucial, but you cannot settle the direction at the beginning and simply pursue it. Focus is something that comes alive through the other elements. It gets shaped and reshaped by the interactive forces of collaboration, deep learning, and accountable actions. Focus gets clearer and more shared as a process of deliberate action evolves.

Second, cultivating collaborative cultures is at the heart of system transformation. This second component clarifies the relationship of teamwork vis-à-vis individualism and the role collaboration plays in producing both strong groups and individuals. But collaboration as an end in itself is a waste of time. Groups are powerful, which means that they can be powerfully wrong. Getting together without the discipline and specificity of collective deliberation can be a grand waste of time. We show how developing collaborative cultures is careful and precise work and has profound impact when carried out well because increasing social capital improves coherence, which in turn attracts newcomers and feeds forward into better results.

Third, the agenda must tackle deepening learning, and this component addresses the relationship of pedagogy and technology. Traditional schooling is increasingly boring for students and for teachers, yet the solution of buying technology has failed to have significant impact. New pedagogies—new learning partnerships between and among students, teachers, and families—are rapidly emerging. Such learning is revolutionizing learning outcomes and their measurement, related to what can be called the 6Cs: communication, critical thinking, collaboration, creativity, character, and citizenship. Crucially, the development of new pedagogies and their link to deep learning outcomes are being accelerated by digital innovations. We ourselves are immersed with districts and schools in this work that we call "the Stratosphere agenda" (see Fullan, 2013c) and New Pedagogies for Deep Learning (NPDL) (www.NPDL.global; 2014). This focus on deepening learning uses pedagogy as the driver with technology as an accelerator. The challenge for schools, districts, and states is to manage their need for continuous improvement of foundational skills, while identifying and supporting innovation to foster new learning outcomes. This will be part of our chapter on deep learning.

Fourth, we think we have a solution for the big bugbear—securing accountability. It is, as you know, public enemy number one as the chief wrong driver. But you can't have a public education system absent of accountability. In our original description of wrong drivers, we cast the wrong driver of negative accountability versus capacity building. Now that we have moved to operationalize the right drivers in action, we see that the proper symmetry should have been "internal accountability versus external accountability."

Thus, the fourth component, securing accountability, is based on developing internal capacity to be effective, to be responsible within the group or system (internal accountability), and to respond to and engage system priorities and performance therein (external accountability). The road to securing accountability is through developing capacity within the group. We show how the first three components of our model put us in a position to secure accountability by leading with internal accountability within the group, and reinforcing it with external accountability.

The core of the framework is "Leadership for Coherence," which links all four components. Leaders working in partnership with others determine how to combine the four components to meet the varying needs of their context—how to make the four "gel" and increase coherence. The coherence making model—its four components in action—must (oddly enough) be pursued *coherently.* Our framework is a dynamic model that ramifies, making the whole greater than the sum of its parts. Master it, and you and your colleagues will be amply rewarded.

Get the Right Mind-Set for Action

Success is not a matter of working your way through the four components of the framework. You have to have the right mind-set. You have to respect what we know about the change process. Here is a good basic definition: *Effective change processes shape and reshape good ideas as they build capacity and ownership among participants.* There are two components: the quality of the idea and the quality of the process. Neglect one or the other and you will fail. And as you see by the definition, things change as you work with them. It was Kurt Lewin who said "if you really want to understand something try changing it." So, have a deep respect for the unpredictability of change.

There is not one surefire way to go about it. Susan Moore Johnson, Geoff Marietta, Monica Higgins, Karen Mapp, and Allen Grossman (2015) studied five school districts reported in their book, *Achieving Coherence in District Improvement.* Three districts—Aldine, Texas; Montgomery County, Maryland; and Long Beach, California—were relatively centralized. Two—Baltimore City Schools and Charlotte-Mecklenburg, North Carolina—were following a path of relative decentralization. All five districts were achieving some success. Even though the five were following different pathways, there were fundamental commonalities. All worked hard on district-schools partnership and trust. All paid attention to lateral relationships between and among schools.

All needed to focus on and figure out the relationship among "programming, budgeting and staffing." All needed to understand and continually engage the culture of their districts and the changing dynamics of their external environments. The essential ingredient for success, says Johnson and her colleagues (2015), was "whether a district could effectively implement whatever theory of change [with the common elements we have identified] it chose" (p. 20). Further, "policies and practices succeeded when they were continuously informed by the knowledge, skills, and experiences of educators from all levels of the system" (p. 49).

Andy Hargreaves, Alan Boyle, and Alma Harris (2014), in their study of especially effective organizations in three sectors—business, education, and sport—identify key characteristics of what they call *uplifting leadership.* Their conclusions have much in common with our framework, but a particularly salient one was the finding that these highly successful organizations learned from the success of others but never tried to imitate what others did. Instead, they found *their own pathway to success.* They did many of the right things, and they learned and adjusted as they proceeded.

The bottom line in our book is this: use our framework, but find your own pathway!

To get you started, review Infographic 1 on Coherence Making.

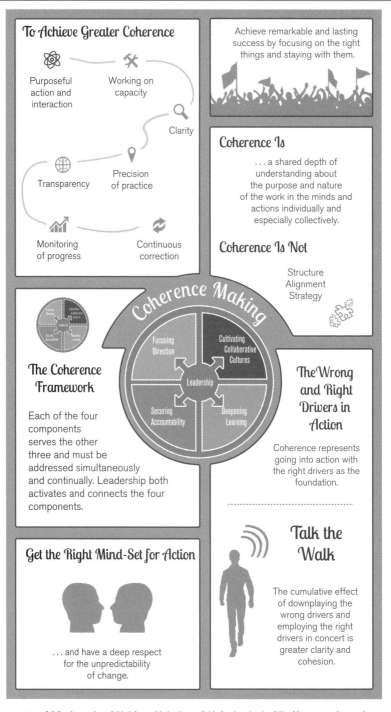

To Achieve Greater Coherence

Purposeful action and interaction

Working on capacity

Clarity

Transparency

Precision of practice

Monitoring of progress

Continuous correction

Achieve remarkable and lasting success by focusing on the right things and staying with them.

Coherence Is

. . . a shared depth of understanding about the purpose and nature of the work in the minds and actions individually and especially collectively.

Coherence Is Not

Structure
Alignment
Strategy

Coherence Making

Focusing Direction

Cultivating Collaborative Cultures

Leadership

Securing Accountability

Deepening Learning

The Coherence Framework

Each of the four components serves the other three and must be addressed simultaneously and continually. Leadership both activates and connects the four components.

The Wrong and Right Drivers in Action

Coherence represents going into action with the right drivers as the foundation.

Talk the Walk

The cumulative effect of downplaying the wrong drivers and employing the right drivers in concert is greater clarity and cohesion.

Get the Right Mind-Set for Action

. . . and have a deep respect for the unpredictability of change.

A full-color version of this infographic is also available for download at **http://www.corwin.com/books/Book244044** under "About" and then "Sample Materials and Chapters."

2

Focusing Direction

Leaders need to find the glue that will increase the coherence of the district and school efforts at every level and build a clear path to improve learning in demonstrable ways. One component of the "glue" is the ability to develop and sustain focused direction in the face of competing and complex demands internally and externally.

The first right driver of the Coherence Framework is *focusing direction.* Leaders need to combine the four elements of focused direction, *purpose driven, goals that impact, clarity of strategy,* and *change leadership,* if they are to meet the changing contexts they face (see Figure 2.1). In this chapter, we examine each of the four elements of focused direction in turn and then provide several examples of focused direction in action.

Purpose Driven

Leaders need the ability to develop a shared moral purpose and meaning as well as a pathway for attaining that purpose. The moral imperative focuses on deep learning for all children regardless of background or circumstance (Fullan, 2010, 2011b). Commitment to the moral imperative of education for all would seem to be a natural fit for public schools. But it doesn't work that way. Having a moral imperative doesn't mean much if you are not getting somewhere. In the absence of progress, educators lose heart—or never develop it in the first place. Of course, some do maintain their moral drive, but it is against all odds. Humans need to experience success to keep going; they need to understand and experience the conditions that advance the cause. In many situations, constant overload and fragmentation overwhelm moral purpose. The development of purpose

Figure 2.1   Focusing Direction

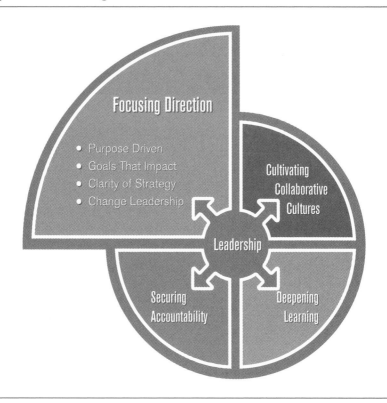

and the other three elements of focused direction is a *process* as much as it is a state. The challenge is to turn chaos into focus. Hargreaves, Boyle, and Harris (2014) call this critical component "dreaming with determination"—a deep, relentless purpose accompanied by an equally strong learning mode.

How Does This Happen?

Leaders must first understand their own moral purpose and be able to combine personal values, persistence, emotional intelligence, and resilience. This is essential because their moral purpose will be reflected in all their decisions and actions.

To clarify your own moral imperative, consider your answers to four questions:

1. What is my moral imperative?

2. What actions do I take to realize this moral imperative?

3. How do I help others clarify their moral imperative?

4. Am I making progress in realizing my moral purpose with students?

Fostering moral imperative in others is not about giving inspirational speeches. Effective leaders foster moral purpose when they do the following:

- Build relationships with everyone, including those who disagree, are skeptical, or even cynical.
- Listen and understand the perspective of others.
- Demonstrate respect for all.
- Create conditions to connect others around that purpose.
- Examine with staff evidence of progress.

Great leaders connect others to the reasons they became educators— their moral purpose. They make purpose part of the organization's DNA by creating opportunities for people to make meaning of the possibilities, work on aspects of the challenge, and achieve success. From working together, they build a deeper understanding of their shared moral purpose, a common language for communicating more effectively, and deeper commitment. However, by itself, moral imperative is not a strategy, so leaders will only realize their moral imperative by developing a small number of actionable and shared goals. Then they learn and build capacity and commitment through purposeful doing.

Goals That Impact What Matters Most

The problem is not the absence of goals in districts and schools today but the presence of too many that are ad hoc, unconnected, and ever-changing. Multiple mandates from states and districts combine with the allure of grants and innovations, resulting in overload and fragmentation. The overload results from too many goals, projects, and initiatives. Even if they are good ideas, the sheer volume makes it impossible for people to manage in a way that gives depth. The second problem is fragmentation. Even when the goals are the right ones, they may not be experienced as connected ideas by the users. People see them as discrete demands with little or no connection to each other or their daily work; scrambling to implement too many directions and lacking a coherent sense of how they connect results in paralysis and frustration.

You can either remain a victim of these—one can almost say natural circumstances in complex society—or you can turn the tables. One could easily say that the bigger system should "get its act together," but don't hold your breath. Our framework and the ideas within enable you to take greater control. You can achieve success under current conditions, as we will shortly show. And if enough of you do it, the system will change.

We illustrate with three districts that operate within the same political, funding, and demographic constraints as neighboring school districts yet manage to provide coherent direction and consistent results for their students. York Region District School Board in Ontario, Canada, has over 200 schools. It created instructional coherence and corresponding individual and collective capacity with a decade-long focus on literacy, resulting in substantial gains for students. The literacy focus guided all decisions, was a beacon for assessing needs and successes, and ensured a common language and knowledge base for everyone.

We see similar patterns in Garden Grove Unified (Knudson, 2013) and Long Beach Unified (Mourshed, Chijioke, & Barber, 2010) in California, where both districts have sustained a consistent, clear focus and strategy for instructional improvement with persistence, despite political, budget, and demographic changes. The solution lies in developing limited goals, persisting, and avoiding distractors. In other words, these leaders turned the table on overload and fragmentation to establish continuous focused direction.

In 2014, the York Region District School Board appointed a new director (superintendent). Although the appointment was from within the district, the new director has a mandate to revisit and renew the vision. We are currently working with the York Region District School Board as they develop an updated vision and direction for the next period. It will need to be focused, inspiring, and engaging for students and educators at all levels of the system.

As we think about York Region and other districts at the early stage of developing a new direction, we note one of the most important change insights we have learned about visioning and coherence. It is a mistake to overload the front end with massive amounts of input from all constituencies *in the absence of action.* It is much more effective to shorten the front-end process and overload, so to speak, by implementing action, learning from it, and grounding the vision in practice. Once again, it is learning by purposeful doing that counts most.

In another large district, we work with (240 schools, high English-language learner [ELL] needs, and huge diversity), we see the promising struggles in action to overcome a history of fragmented overload. The district has achieved success for students but over the years has initiated a myriad of programs, projects, and initiatives to meet the changing needs of its population. Principals and teachers are proud of the district but describe feeling overwhelmed and unsure what the real priorities are when there are so many. The district recognizes that future success depends on a much clearer focus. This scenario of overload and fragmentation is not uncommon and could be happening in any state, province, or district. Figuring out what the small number of ambitious goals ought to be and staying focused on them is a challenge. This means reducing the number of goals and strategies, giving people experiences that show the integration (not just coordination) of the goals and strategies, learning as you go, and constantly reiterating the direction and how well you are progressing. Talking the walk is what we call this process.

We recommend a four-step approach to tackling what we have called the problem of "initiativitis."

1. Be Transparent

Acknowledge and get clarity on the issue. Consider quick, transparent assessment methods (surveys, focus groups, interviews) to identify the perceptions of staff, leaders, school board members, students, parents, and community.

Avoid excuses and blame. Review the data, and avoid the "yeah, but" syndrome. Establish norms that resist the blame game of "overload is because of xyz's focus while my initiative is essential." Remember that the projects and initiatives were likely implemented as solid approaches to a perceived need at the time. The problem is not the quality but the cumulative effect, volume, overlap, and lack of clarity or connections. Be careful not to have a lengthy front-end process.

2. Build a Collaborative Approach

Recognize that finding solutions to complex problems requires the intelligence and talents of everyone. Create a task team that is small but representative of the layers of the organization to strategize a plan and provide leadership.

The senior leadership team must develop a common language and approach that is sustained and communicated consistently across the system. All parts of the organization, including unions, classified staff, students, and parents, must feel they have a place in the process. Collaboration during initial and ongoing implementation is especially crucial.

3. Develop a Clear Strategy: Reduce, Reframe, Remove

Reduce the clutter and overload by listing (on sticky notes, for example) and examining current initiatives with a view to reducing and clustering them:

- Avoid the temptation of trying to realign them or cluster them into a new picture of the old way. Start with student learning. Ask, "What learning do we want for our students?" instead of starting with, for example, "How do we implement the Common Core State Standards (CCSS)?"
- Identify the umbrella focus that captures this vision. It may be 21st century learning, literate learners, college and career readiness, literacy, or others. The process needs to be inclusive enough to involve everyone.
- Name the two or three ambitious goals you will need to pursue if you want to attain this vision.

- Develop a strategy for achieving the goals. Identify the supports that are needed. Do not just try to fit all the current programs and initiatives under the new goals. Rather, identify what is needed and review current projects or supports to determine fit.

Reframe the connections between the goals to overcome fragmentation:

- At this stage, the designers or task team may see the connections and overall plan, but it does not have meaning for the users. You need to develop a coherent picture, visually and in words, of the pieces and how they connect.

Remove distractors, which may be mandates or alluring innovations:

- Identify the time wasters and inefficiencies. These are often management issues that take time away from the learning focus and keep the system off balance. For example, the Hawaii Department of Education created a task team with the goal of reducing by 25 percent the paperwork, forms, and demands on school leader time to support leaders in focusing on literacy. Within three months, they had reduced the requirements by almost 50 percent by identifying duplication across departments, data collected but not used, and other inefficiencies. This sent a strong message to the field that they were serious about focused direction.
- Give leaders permission to say no. Once the goals and strategy are clearly understood and manageable, leaders have a rationale for saying no to the multitude of requests that bombard schools and districts.
- Avoid shiny objects and other alluring possibilities. Distractors can be very useful and effective projects, initiatives, or supports. The key is in discerning the relevance of the new addition to the goals and current strategy. It may be a great innovation—just not at this time.

Kirtman and Fullan (2015) have a chapter on "moving compliance to the side of the plate." The idea is not to be a rebel for the sake of it but to change the game from compliance to purposeful focus.

4. Cultivate Engagement

Communicate often, and listen even more often. Avoid overreliance on print or digital media, and instead, engage all groups with the goals and strategy, allowing rich conversations to develop meaning for everyone. Use social media to reinforce these discussions. Cycles of sharing and revision will lead to a common language about the direction, deeper understanding, and commitment.

Build opportunities to check with all groups regularly over time—for example, assistant superintendents can begin all main meetings with principals or schools by articulating the goals and strategy (we witnessed this in York Region; it takes fewer than 10 minutes) then checking progress by asking the following: What is going well? What do we need to be worrying about or taking action on? Giving an authentic forum for consistent, meaningful conversation about the goals and the strategy will reinforce the common language and understanding of the direction as well as build ownership for results.

Once the purpose and goals are identified, it is critical that everyone perceive that there is a clear strategy for achieving them and be able to see their part in that strategy. People need to get better and better at "talking the walk."

Clarity of Strategy

Clarity and coherence are not just about goals; crucially, they are also about strategy. Clarity is subjective—is it clear in people's minds and actions? Can people talk the walk with ease and specificity? We define coherence as a shift in *shared mind-set* rather than alignment, which is about getting the structures right. Alignment on paper does not generate clarity. New cultures do. For example, a district or school could use the steps just given in the last section and create a set of goals and strategy that was carefully aligned on paper. The strategies and resources could be conceptually linked to the goals. None of this will give participants the experiences and capacity to become clear on what it means in practice (in this sense, clarity follows capacity more than it precedes it). In other words, developing new skills (capacities)—especially with others—*increases* clarity and, in turn, commitment. Getting traction on coherence in whole system change means building purposeful and continuous interaction over time with an expectation for all schools to improve learning for all students. Clarity, thus, precedes coherence.

As we stated in Chapter 1, successful change processes are a function of shaping and reshaping good ideas as they build capacity and ownership. This can be demonstrated by cross-connecting explicitness (the ideas) with change climate (the change process) as we do in Figure 2.2. Coherence becomes a function of the interplay between the growing explicitness of the idea and the change culture.

Figure 2.2 Change Quality Quadrant

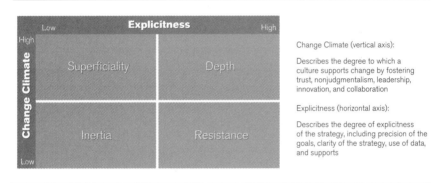

Change Climate (vertical axis):

Describes the degree to which a culture supports change by fostering trust, nonjudgmentalism, leadership, innovation, and collaboration

Explicitness (horizontal axis):

Describes the degree of explicitness of the strategy, including precision of the goals, clarity of the strategy, use of data, and supports

Let's examine the four combinations and the results.

Superficiality

Starting with the top left-hand quadrant—low explicitness and a good climate—people are getting along okay, but they are not doing much. We call it superficiality. If the strategy for improvement is not precise, actionable, and clear, we may see activity but at very superficial levels.

Inertia

In many ways, the bottom left-hand quadrant represents the history of the teaching profession—behind the classroom door, where teachers left each other alone. What this means is that teachers had a license to be creative, but they also had a license to be ineffective (and perhaps not even know it). In the former case, innovative teachers receive little feedback on their ideas, nor do these ideas become available to others. In the case of isolated, less than effective teachers, they get little help to improve. We call this inertia—people keep on doing what they are already doing.

Resistance

The bottom right quadrant is also interesting because in this scenario policy makers and others have invested in developing specific innovations (or they buy detailed programs off the shelf)—perhaps with a high degree of explicitness—but they insufficiently involved teachers in developing ownership and new capacities. If the programs in question are sound, they can result in some gains in the short run (tightening an otherwise loose system), but because teachers have not been engaged in shaping the ideas or the strategy the innovation wanes due to lack of ownership. When conditions for change are weak, there is low trust or collaboration; therefore, there is little willingness to innovate or take risks. When this is combined with a very directive strategy that makes heavy demands or mandates, resistance and pushback escalate.

Depth

The optimal environment combines a strong climate for change with an explicitness of strategy. When people are operating in conditions of high trust, collaboration, and effective leadership, they are more willing to innovate and take risks. If we balance that with a strategy that has precision, clarity, and measures of success, we see changes implemented with depth and impact. We will see more of this in Chapter 4 on deepening learning.

This organizer builds on and extends the concept of flow that suggests that optimal experience occurs when challenges are balanced with skills (Csikszentmihalyi, 2008). We propose that organizations need to find this intersection of high explicitness and strong ownership if they are to challenge and engage high performance. This takes a coherent force of leadership at all levels to set and sustain the new direction and to create the conditions to support growth. At the district level, this may be a coalition of 3 to 20 (depending on the size of the district) key leaders who interact continually to have a similar grasp of the core goals as well as the strategies that will be used to implement them. At the school level, teams of teachers and principals play a vital role in designing implementation strategies, building capacity, and monitoring progress. The interplay between a strong climate for change and an explicit strategy for achieving the goals promotes and sustains trust, communication, connectedness, and meaningful work.

Change Leadership

The pace and complexity of innovation and change today—combined with the emergence of instant digital connections—is shifting our notions of an effective change process to a much more fluid dynamic. Leaders remain crucial in creating a North Star for action, establishing enabling conditions, and shaping a pathway for change; however, the new process of change shifts from a notion of sequential, discrete stages of the traditional alignment of policy, resources, skill development, and supports (getting the pieces aligned) to a more organic process of diffusion and continuous learning. Under these conditions, the ultimate question is this: How do we help people through the change process and get greater coherence while we are at it? This is the sophistication of change leadership.

It has long been stated that change is a process, not an event. The leader's role is to manage the transition from the current to the future state. We use a metaphor of two fishbowls to describe the challenge of shifting individuals and organizations from current to future practice (see Figure 2.3).

The difficulty of shifting practice or moving from bowl to bowl is compounded by two additional factors of confidence and competence. Some do not believe they have the ability to make the leap from what they know to the new way of thinking and doing. Even if they are good swimmers in the current bowl, they do not know if they have the skills to make the leap or be swimmers in the new way. They lack confidence to make the leap. The question of competence is a closely related problem. Some are not good swimmers or leapers and are fearful for good reason; others may not have the skills to swim in the new way of thinking

Figure 2.3 Shifting Practice

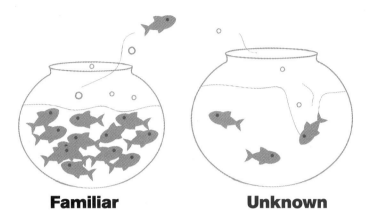

Familiar

As we consider the bowl on the left, most fish feel comfortable in their bowl because they are familiar with their circumstances, even though they may be dissatisfied.

The expectations of the kind of swimming are traditional and known.

The level of collaboration is the status quo—they know who is in the bowl and how to interact.

The current rewards are understood, and they know how to survive.

Unknown

Contrast that with the bowl on the right, which is full of unknowns.

The expectations of the kind of leaping and swimming required in the new bowl are unclear.

Collaboration is not yet established, so they have few friends or colleagues and the support structures are unknown.

Rewards are distant and often lack specificity while the dangers of leaping are in the present.

---

and doing. One can see for both confidence and competence that both capacity building and a supportive climate are crucial. Effective change leaders know that.

The fishbowl metaphor provides clues to how we support others to shift practice:

- Foster clarity of the purpose for the leap and specificity of the destination.
- Support the early leapers, and learn from their attempts.
- Build the capacity of others to leap with support.
- Create a culture of collaboration where leaping can be nurtured.
- Recognize successes at leaping at all points of the journey.

We don't want to carry the metaphor too far, but it underscores one final issue: we need to make the journey of change vivid for people—bring it to life. Connect it to what they know (the simple fishbowl example) as a catalyst to have honest conversations about their worries, desires for change, and their needs for support.

We have learned a great deal about the ins and outs of change leadership by working with leading practitioners. Such leaders understand and foster the new change dynamic where progress is not linear. The big findings are as follows:

- The best leaders use the new change dynamic to move their organizations forward and "participate as learners."
- They balance and integrate push and pull strategies.
- They build vertical and horizontal capacity and integration.

1. The New Change Dynamic

Managing the transition in this complex change environment calls for a more fluid change process dynamic, which is detailed in Figure 2.4.

Directional Vision

Directional vision emerges from working in partnership to develop a shared purpose and vision and by engaging in continuous collaborative conversations that build shared language, knowledge, and expectations.

Figure 2.4 The New Change Process

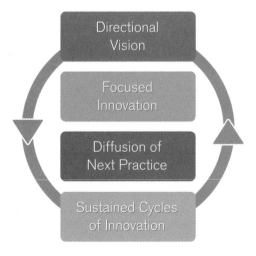

Leaders play an essential role in continuously defining, articulating, and shaping a pathway for the new vision. In such rapidly changing times, it's not about prescribing every nuance of the journey but about setting the overarching direction and establishing the enabling conditions that foster growth and innovation. As the group collaborates on the work, they internalize the concepts, share stories of success, and build commitment.

Focused Innovation

As leaders try to manage innovations such as implementation of the CCSS combined with the emergence of the digital world in classrooms, we are seeing a more rapid prototyping similar to that described in the "lean startup" strategy (Ries, 2011). The ability to connect deeply across schools, districts, and even globally means that more ideas are bubbling up and can be cross-germinated and refined. The catalyst for shifting practices can come from anywhere in the organization. Strong leaders and organizations seek out the early innovations and support them. They invite innovation, make it okay to make mistakes as long as people learn from them, and recognize early attempts in order to learn from them. As Andreas Mayer, the principal at W. G. Davis School in Ontario, said, "We need to take two steps back to go three steps forward." Lean start-up theory would tell us that the first versions of the new way will likely be inferior, but if we recount stories of the early innovations, it brings visibility to the work and provides powerful learning that is contagious and leads ultimately to a better version. What is important at this stage is not the regimentation of traditional implementation with a single pathway, mandatory capacity building, and compliance. Leaders need to set the directional vision, allow experimentation connected to the vision, put in mechanisms for learning from the work, and then establish ways to share the promising approaches across the organization.

Diffusion of Next Practice

As new ideas and approaches emerge, organizations need not only to build capacity but also to cultivate intentional ways to learn from the work—to share these more strategically and pull the threads of promising practices together to make them visible to everyone.

At the diffusion phase, schools and districts need to develop expertise to do the following:

- Cultivate multiple internal sources of innovation.
- Support safe places for risk taking.
- Build capacity vertically and laterally across the organization.
- Provide opportunities for deeper collaboration within and across schools.
- Develop mechanisms to make and share collective insights and knowledge.

Building capacity is a key lever for change. It needs a clear focus connected to student learning, effective practices, and sustained cycles of learning. More and more, the capacity building needs are bubbling up from the organization once the enabling conditions are in place. Here are two examples of the new change dynamic from districts with which we are working:

Pittsburg Unified District in California needed to introduce the CCSS to build a common language and understanding of the changes ahead. Rather than hire consultants or use internal experts, their innovative approach was to select 85 teachers from the district and give them the task, time, and resources to design a learning experience for a common professional day for all teachers in the district at the opening of the year. This approach sent very strong messages to the system that as a district we do the following:

- Will collaborate to learn about this innovation together
- Value our teachers' expertise
- Trust the professionalism of staff

Pittsburg is part of a collaborative that brings together school leadership teams four times annually from across the district. In a recent session, teachers shared that they are seeing remarkable developments in their students' level of thinking in just a few months as they shift from teaching answers to helping students ask their questions. They say this is much harder work than in previous years but are energized by the gains they are seeing as students flourish. They are comfortable in sharing both their challenges and successes across the schools, which then serves to raise the bar for everyone while seeding next practices. The enabling conditions of trust, lateral and vertical transparency, and capacity building create impetus for schools to take the lead.

A second example of diffusion emerges from a high school, one of 240 schools in the Peel District School Board in Ontario, Canada.

At Central Peel High School, we filmed teachers of this high school serving a diverse population, who talked about identifying problems three years ago when graduation rates were falling, enrollment was declining, disruptive behavior was on the rise, and students were apathetic. The staff spent time searching for solutions and eventually decided that the students needed an environment that was more engaging and in tune with their world outside the classroom. Despite feeling very unsure of how to shift their ways, the school instituted a bring your own device (BYOD) policy. The principal, Lawrence DeMaeyer, established a "culture of yes" where there was freedom to try new things without judgment. Some teachers were further along the journey than others and began sharing expertise by modeling apps and technologies. The technology committee grew from eight members to thirty as interest surged and the focus shifted rapidly from devices to pedagogy as the driver. Within two years, they saw an increase in retention rates, multiple measures of student engagement, and a revitalized staff. By year two, the district also moved to a BYOD policy, and opportunities for resources and capacity building began to increase. Once again, we see great movement evolving from directional vision combined with freedom to innovate and intentional mechanisms to share the learning. (Video available at www.michaelfullan.ca.)

Sustained Cycles of Innovation

Once positive change gets moving, the challenge is how to sustain it. We recognize that the cycle will never be finished in a rapidly changing world. Leading for an unknown future means that leaders must foster cycles of innovation by attracting and selecting talent, providing a culture of trust and exploration, synthesizing the learning gleaned from the innovation, providing communication pathways vertically and horizontally in the organization, and celebrating each step of the evolving journey. This not only fosters current growth but also reinforces the cycles of innovation by building on the emerging knowledge and creating an environment of ever reaching potential.

2. Balance Push and Pull Strategies

Great leaders read situations and people. They build strong relationships and seek feedback from all sources. These attributes give them insight into when to push or be assertive and when they need to draw people in or follow. The best leaders use push and pull in combination.

One illustrative example is from Peters Elementary School in Garden Grove Unified, serving 650 PreK–3 students, 77 percent ELLs, 56 percent Latino, 21 percent Vietnamese, and 81 percent free or reduced lunch. The principal, Michelle Pinchot, recounts arriving at the school and taking a few months to listen carefully to teachers, students, and parents. She realized that many of the students could not read and gave herself five years to create the culture and structures that would improve learning for students. Michelle was careful to build relationships first but not get bogged down in this process; in fact, once there is some initial rapport, the best way to develop deeper relationships is *through purposeful action.*

The first push strategy was confronting the data, acknowledging that their students could do better, and eliminating the excuses based on student background and circumstance. The second push strategy was to create three teams: the first for management issues, the second for data, and the third for curriculum and instruction. The principal sat on all three teams and worked alongside the teachers on issues (participated as a learner). The pull strategy was that the teachers determined the specific purposes of each of the teams and were invited to participate. The number of teachers volunteering to serve has risen every year. When we filmed in the school last year, it was apparent that the teams have taken responsibility for their mandates. Team members are proud of their contributions, and all of them could easily articulate the goals and strategy they were taking to achieve improved learning. Student results in reading have climbed, reaching double-digit increases (11 percent) for the first time ever. The principal and a growing number of teacher-leaders were able to master the push and pull of using the teams as a lever for improvement through a clear directional vision (all of our students will read), enabling conditions (collaborative teams), forums for meaningful interaction, and capacity building. (Video available at www.michaelfullan.ca.)

3. Build Vertical and Lateral Capacity and Integration

Change leaders are intentional in developing relationships, shared understanding, and mutual accountability vertically (at every level of the organization) and horizontally (across schools, departments, and divisions). The catalyst is mobilizing meaningful joint work and learning from that work. As groups go deeper into solution finding, they become clearer about purpose and strengthen commitment to the goals. Focused vertical and lateral interaction over time fosters greater shared coherence.

Let's return to York Region District School Board to examine how in their first phase they combined purpose, goals, clarity of strategy, and change knowledge to build districtwide coherence that fostered sustained improvement and focus. Such coherence, as we have said, must be both vertical (between schools and the district) and horizontal (across schools as peers).

Clear Purpose and Goals

York Region's overarching purpose was literacy defined broadly to include cultivating critical thinking, problem solving, and communication across all grades and content areas. The goal was sustained relentlessly for 10 years and augmented by the use of assessment data and instructional strategies. Every staff member could see his or her place in the goal.

Explicit Strategy

The Literacy Collaborative was established as a key lever for capacity building. Leadership teams from every school composed of the principal and three to seven teachers met face-to-face four times annually to build internal capacity and connect with school teams and the broader district strategy.

Continuous interaction and *learning vertically and laterally* across the district developed a common language and knowledge base about literacy and change. This evolved to talking the walk—when any member of the district could articulate the goals and strategy of the school and its connection to the district in a meaningful way.

Explicitness of the strategy was reinforced because all 24 assistant super-intendents were involved in the Literacy Collaborative, and decision making and structures were aligned with the overall focus on literacy.

Change Leadership

A strong culture of learning was fostered across the district. The superintendent, Bill Hogarth, modeled being the lead learner by taking the first few minutes of every Literacy Collaborative session to revisit the goals and strategy but always shared an example of implementation from his school visits or a perspective that deepened and extended understanding. His consistent messaging and investment into going deeper were compelling.

Lateral and vertical interaction and learning became the glue for coherence in York Region.

As we mentioned previously, York Region is now undertaking the development of a renewed vision. There are a few lessons to be learned here. First, achieved coherence, which they had, does not last forever (i.e., times change, innovation presses). Second, the new process must similarly be collaborative with the people who are there—a group that is a mixture of newcomers and incumbents. Third, in this renewal process, York can draw on its existing capacity to leverage itself forward in forging a renewed directional vision.

Focused Direction in Action

Two more case examples will help to illustrate how focused direction operates over time in large systems. We take a look at a provincial system and a high-poverty urban district.

The Ontario Story

The challenge of achieving high levels of quality and equity in public education across entire districts, states, or countries is emerging as a priority across the globe. Three prominent international agencies, including the Organisation for Economic Cooperation and Development (OECD) (2011), the McKinsey Group (Mourshed, Chijioke, & Barber, 2010), and the National Center for Education (NCEE) and the Economy in the United States (Tucker, 2011), have identified Ontario as a powerful example of a government deliberately setting out to improve the whole system and having the results to show for it. The last decade has seen Ontario rise in the Program for International Student Assessment (PISA) rankings and to be named one of the highest-performing and most improved education systems in the world (Mourshed et al., 2010). The Ontario experience offers an important example for other countries—and especially its neighbor the United States—as it has done so with similar demographics and a system that is larger in size than 45 of the U.S. states (Herman, 2013).

Using a focused capacity building strategy linked to all schools and districts, there have been significant gains in literacy, numeracy, and high school graduation rates. International researchers and visitors note consistently the high degree of coherence of the educational system, which is reflected in consistency of good practice and a shared understanding of the priorities and reform strategies across all levels (Fullan, 2010). District school board leaders, unions, teachers, and principals are able to explain with specificity what they are doing and why—the strategy behind the action and the results. By maintaining a consistent focus on its three core priorities as it developed capacity and ownership at all levels of the system, what started out as the government's agenda became the system's agenda—a shared ownership that binds and holds everyone accountable to each other and to the larger system.

Ontario is Canada's largest province with a population of over 13 million, serving a diverse student population of over two million children, and 27 percent of students have parents whose first language is not English (a percentage that is much larger in an urban area like York Region). Ontario has 4,000 elementary and 900 secondary schools operated through 72 local school districts, and 95 percent of all students attend one of the four publicly funded systems. Despite its large and diverse student population, Ontario has consistently performed well on international tests, including PISA, and has shown consistent, sustainable growth on its own provincial measures. In the last decade, the percentage of students reaching the ambitious provincial standard of level 3 in literacy has increased by almost 20 percent, and during the same period, high school graduation rates increased 25 percent. Furthermore, important student gaps have been reduced, such as reducing the gap between special education students and peers by 8 percent and ELLs and their counterparts. As well, the percentage of students performing at level 1 has decreased from 17 percent to less than 6 percent. Across the 900 high schools, graduation rates have climbed from a base of 68 percent to 84 percent.

How do you get such a focused, sustained direction across a whole system? The *right drivers*, a *capacity building approach,* and what we call "leadership from the middle" (LFTM) are at the core of the Ontario story of whole system change (for the latest account of the Ontario story, see Fullan & Rincón-Gallardo, in press).

To understand the depth of the shift, it is important to examine the context and history of the province. The government holding power from 1995 to 2003 led with the *wrong drivers*: intent on massive budget cuts; punitive accountability; and fostering public dissatisfaction with public schools, while blaming teachers. The resulting performance was characterized by stagnated student achievement, labor disruptions, and low teacher morale (Glaze, Mattingley, & Andrews, 2013; Sattler, 2012). In contrast, in 2003, a new government took office with a platform to make the renewal of public education one of its highest priorities. Their strategy built on the pockets of innovation and expertise that existed across the province and used a capacity building strategy to build partnerships with educators and parents to improve learning. What differentiates Ontario's approach from so many others is the widely shared ownership of the reform agenda on the part of teachers, schools, and district school board leaders.

As we examine the strategy in more detail, it is important to note that the seeds of change began to flourish long before 2003. Beginning in the 1990s, a handful of districts were providing cutting-edge leadership in whole system change (put another way, these districts were ahead of the system). They developed the prototypes of what we now call school leadership teams, sustained learning institutes for leadership, and capacity building models that built both vertical and horizontal capacity. These districts focused on increasing instructional precision, literacy, and supporting schools to be the drivers of change, not the recipient of fragmented mandates. These districts realized that they had no consistent way of measuring results, so they formed a collaborative of 11 districts to develop an accountability system that would be nonpunitive and based on authentic student performances. They created processes for appraisal that were focused on cycles of growth, not checklists. Four districts formed a consortium with the University of Toronto and not only built knowledge but also created provincewide forums for sharing that knowledge laterally.

This LFTM (district level) was seeding innovation, building expertise, and reaching upward to influence the policy level. When a "wrong driver government" (to use our language) was elected in 1995, intent on control and reducing budgets, not building capacity, these innovative districts and leaders faced a hostile environment. Since formal mechanisms for sharing their expertise across districts were limited, their impact remained in pockets. The capacity that had been built remained, so leaders continued to innovate internally but kept under the radar. Once the new government came to power in 2003, there was strong LFTM available from these innovative districts to support the new policy directions. In 2003, the new government and its Ministry of Education did not have the credibility with the field nor the internal capacity to implement their agenda for renewal. Thus, they built strong partnerships and leveraged the talent and leadership that existed in districts to build their credibility and capacity to achieve the goals.

Several bold actions created a new culture based on respect, trust, mutual goals, and an infrastructure of sustained support. The strategy incorporated features of the Coherence Framework: focused direction, collaborative cultures, focus on capacity building and learning, and transparent but nonpunitive accountability.

First, the focus was clearly stated with a provincial policy agenda shaped around three ambitious goals that were "sticky," as they were clear to educators, parents, and community alike and sustained for more than a decade:

- Increase literacy and numeracy proficiency and high school graduation rates.
- Reduce the achievement gap for subgroups (ELLs, special education, schools in poverty) relative to the three core achievement goals.
- Build public confidence in schools.

Support from the government was unwavering and honed by a core group of leaders who monitored the implementation strategy. They ensured that the focus was sustained and supported, starting with a financial commitment of $2.6 billion to be added back to the system during the government's first four-year term. Another key element of the focused direction strategy involved the creation of a new entity: the Literacy and Numeracy Secretariat (LNS).

This secretariat was staffed by approximately 80 people—a mixture of existing Ministry of Education (state department) staff and the majority through secondments of highly respected leaders borrowed from school districts for three-year terms. LNS focused on the small number of priority goals for the province and worked with the 72 school districts in the province to create focus and related capacity for implementing the priorities. Their role involved building deep relationships with the district leaders to support districts in moving toward their priority goals. The work of the secretariat used a four-lever strategy that focused on improving teaching and learning in the classroom; improving school effectiveness: building leadership capacity; and using cycles of research, monitoring, and evaluation (Gallagher, 2014).

First, the strategy at the elementary level (4,000 schools) largely focused on raising the bar and closing the gap relative to literacy and numeracy. At the secondary level (900 schools), the strategy was called *Student Success/Learning to 18.* This strategy provided for a student success teacher in each high school who mobilized resources to keep track of the progress of every student; provided effective instruction and offered a more explicit and richer menu of pathways and programs for high school completion and postsecondary education; and promoted the well-being of students, including provision of an adult to form caring relationships with individual students (Glaze et al., 2013).

Second, the development of collaborative cultures was a core strategy, including within school collaboration, cross-school and cross-district collaboration, and partnership with LNS and Student Success. No high-performing educational system has been able to improve its performance as a whole system without the support and ownership of the reform agenda by teachers. One of the first steps of the new government was to *develop a culture of respect for teachers as professionals* and engage them in the renewal strategy. Developing labor peace and stability was a necessary step in setting the foundation for ongoing partnership between the government, school districts, and schools and was reinforced when a four-year collective agreement was signed with teacher unions across the province. As well, unions were engaged to support professional learning and provided significant budgets to work in tandem with districts and the government.

Educators were viewed as professional partners, and solutions were sought from the field. Promising practices from the early innovative districts and schools were identified and shared. Teachers were engaged to create exemplars, videos, and resources that were shared widely. This reliance on growth from within, augmented by experts, sent strong messages to teachers and leaders that their input was valued. The answer was not perceived to be in a "program, binder, or app" but rather a solution to be codeveloped.

Third, improving teaching and learning practices was at the heart of the capacity building strategy. Investments were made in collective capacity building related to instruction and leadership. Sustained professional learning, focused on a set of high-yield instructional practices, was offered consistently across the province to create a common language, knowledge base, and skill sets for teachers and leaders. Learning sessions were always followed with application and networks for support. Change was accelerated with the easy accessibility of video exemplars, digital supports, and webinars created by Ontario teachers and leaders. Capacity building was not mandated, but when the quality was so high and so accessible in multiple formats, the diffusion was widespread. At the secondary level, a similar set of high-yield literacy strategies for grades 7–12 were identified. Curriculum teams from each content area were then invited to create resource banks tailored to their content areas. This engagement of expertise from the field ensured that the offerings were relevant and credible, while reinforcing the partnership and goals.

Fourth, Ontario took a different approach to accountability. As we have said, punitive accountability is a wrong driver for educational reform because it does not produce the desired results. Instead, the strategy of capacity building combined with monitoring and supportive development and intervention has been at the core of Ontario's approach. They have avoided using performance data to rank schools or districts based on achievement and do not publicly identify failing schools. Data are used by schools and districts to identify key areas of improvement and to inform further development.

When Ontario identified 800 schools that were considered to be underperforming or stuck, they designed a comprehensive intervention model to provide targeted, nonpunitive, and transparent support, called the Ontario

Focused Intervention Partnership (OFIP). The approach built the collective capacity of teacher teams to better target instructional strategies to meet the needs of their students using a collaborative inquiry model. The results were dramatic with fewer than 100 schools still designated as poor performing after three years of use. Beyond the student results, the strategy sent a clear message to schools that the government was interested in working with them to improve learning. At the secondary level, the Student Success School Support initiative provides differentiated support to high schools where student achievement was below the provincial standard including targeted professional learning sessions for principals and teams with a focus on monitoring data and identifying instructional practices.

As a learning organization, Ontario wanted a deeper understanding of the strategies and conditions that were propelling improvement. Rather than a "Why can't you be more like your brother?" mind-set, they provided an intentional format to capture and share insights. The annual publication *Schools on the Move* featured a range of schools that were further along the journey. Each story was concise with the schools providing insights into what had helped them on the pathway. Programs such as the Teacher Learning and Leadership Program (TLLP), designed for experienced teachers to model and share best practices with other teachers through self-directed, job-embedded professional learning projects were funded and connected teachers and leaders across the system.

We noted previously the recent Ontario case study by Fullan and Rincón-Gallardo (in press), which goes into additional detail with respect to how the small number of goals was explicitly and continuously integrated in all aspects of the strategy. These three core goals in the 2003–2014 period— improving student achievement in literacy, numeracy, and high school graduation; reducing the gap for all students in these achievements; and increasing public confidence in education—are incorporated and reiterated in all aspects of the strategy. They are directly addressed in the work of the LNS as it interacts with districts and schools. As the province develops policies in teacher development, leadership development, use of assessment data, and so on, these additional policies are continually positioned and expressed as related to the three core goals, even though these policies are being developed by other departments and divisions. In fact, they are developed in partnership across divisions and with the education sector (schools and districts).

There is another change lesson here that we foreshadow relative to Chapter 5 on accountability. Instead of placing accountability, standards for teachers and principals, and school improvement plans as front-end requirements, the Ontario strategy developed these areas with the districts, producing some wonderful frameworks and tools—School Effectiveness Framework, District Effectiveness Framework, Ontario Leadership Framework, Teacher Annual Learning Plan, and so on. None of these frameworks are requirements, but virtually everyone uses them—because they have been developed together and because there are normative expectations (pressure if you like) from the system and from peers that they should be used.

As we step back and consider whole system change in perspective, some market-oriented initiatives such as charter schools or Teach for America may be able to improve the chances and outcomes for some students, but none have been successful at simultaneously improving student performance and increasing equity of outcomes for all students. Whole system reform is about improving every school and every district in a province, state, or country, not just some. The Ontario case offers a clear example that whole system change is achievable. Since 2003, following years of stagnation and low morale, the educational system in Ontario has dramatically improved and continues to improve its performance on key measures: increased student achievement, reduced achievement gaps, and increased public confidence in the system.

In summary, these improvements are the result of combining the right drivers:

- Setting a small number of ambitious goals directly related to student achievement
- Fostering collaborative cultures focused on instructional improvement within and across schools as well as between schools and the larger system
- Improving teaching and learning at all levels of the system by using a capacity building approach
- Using transparent and nonpunitive accountability approaches

This combination of the right drivers, partnership, and leveraging LFTM has led to gains in Ontario that are sustainable and dramatic because they have built internal capacity for continuous improvement.

The Garden Grove Story

The second example is the district story of Garden Grove Unified in California and how they have made dramatic gains for students over the past decade. Garden Grove has about 80 schools with just under 50,000 students, serving a diverse student population of 86 percent Latino and Asian students with an average poverty rate of 72 percent. A decade ago, the graduation rate was 24 percent—far below the state with reading and math scores in the lowest percentiles. Ten years later, their graduation rates as well as reading and math scores have surpassed the state, and they out-perform their highest-performing urban peers by demonstrating consistent growth overall and particularly for their minority and poverty students.

A recent report for the California collaborative summarized six interrelated elements that have become part of their culture and strategy (Knudson, 2013):

1. The centrality of teachers and students

2. Coherence

3. Emphasis on relationships

4. Central office service mentality

5. Trust and empowerment

6. Orientation to continuous improvement

In working with Garden Grove, we have seen firsthand how skilled leaders combine the four elements of focused direction.

First, Garden Grove anchors its effort in a sharp and persistent pursuit of core learning goals for all. The focus on student learning is relentless. We often hear the statement "all students can learn," but in Garden Grove, the strategies are designed to make it happen. Combined with the laser-like focus on academic improvement is a profound concern for the well-being and life chances as demonstrated through the robust scholarship program.

Second, the core goals are linked to measurement of impact. The improvement of reading and mathematics and readiness for college and career have been articulated, assessed, monitored, and transparently reviewed as well as have been the subject of capacity building. Overall, Garden Grove has focused on increasing life chances for underperformers and children of poverty. The results show the fruits of this effort. Garden Grove started well below state student achievement averages in the early 2000s, and they are now well above the average.

Third, Garden Grove has developed a strong and clear strategy and culture (called locally "the Garden Grove Way"). It consists of four elements:

1. Continuous improvement of instructional quality and spreading the best instructional practices and ideas to achieve these goals across the system are a relentless focus. Core strategies were identified and consistent support is provided to build expertise at all levels.

2. Building teacher capacity is seen as the route to improvement as articulated by the former superintendent Laura Schwalm: "You're never going to be a better district than your teachers." The selection of core strategies avoided the "pockets of success" problem by using a collective capacity strategy to achieve results. This success has diffused across the district, and with that foundation in place, there is greater trust and empowerment for schools to tackle deeper learning accelerated by technology.

3. The district values its relationships highly and takes great care in recruitment and hiring of the best people and building their capacity through induction, coaching, mentoring, and a lifetime of learning. They nurture the development of existing school leaders and that of teachers on special assignment roles in order to foster instructional capacity across the district.

4. Culture and collaboration are pervasive. People talk proudly of the Garden Grove Way as both the aspiration for quality and a valuing of students and each other. Central office staffing is very lean but very connected to the field. The work is horizontally and vertically connected, creating a seamless culture.

Fourth and finally, development of change leadership has been central to Garden Grove's success. They viewed change as a process and have been persistent in doing the hard work to move all schools, not just some. "If you want to move something that's difficult to move, everyone needs to be pushing in the same direction. It takes more than goals. It takes working on and sharing the strategy day after day" (L. Schwalm, personal communication, 2014). Garden Grove leaders have been careful not to be distracted by the latest education trends, including not seeking grants that they felt would lessen the concentration of core goals. In short, Garden Grove maintained a clear focus on improving instruction, built widely shared engagement, and nurtured capacity.

They have mastered the push and pull strategy. In the early years, the selection of strategies and goals was more directive and "pushy" in order to get results. As capacity has grown, the district is now engaging leaders and teachers in determining next steps. More collaboration is evident in dealing with issues such as common assessment practices and innovations in digital use.

Both vertical and lateral relationships are addressed. Their lean district leadership structure has reinforced the consistency of messaging around goals and strategy and deepened vertical relationships. The emergence of districtwide learning partners for school leaders and the work of teachers on special assignment are examples of redefining relationships and building connections across roles and units.

Final Thoughts

We have shown in this chapter how successful systems have rallied around focused direction, and that focus is not just a matter of having uplifting goals. It is a process involving initial and continuous engagement around core goals persistently pursued. Districts and states that develop focused direction are purpose driven, select a small number of ambitious goals linked to impact, are able to develop clarity of strategy for achieving the goals, and use change knowledge to meet needs tailored to their context. They are focused, and they learn as they go to adapt and deepen their core goals and strategies. Finally, remember that "focusing direction" is never finished. It is always ongoing.

As we delve more deeply into the framework, we have already seen the "cameo" appearance of the three other main elements of the Coherence Framework: cultivating collaborative cultures, deepening learning, and securing accountability. We need to treat each of these elements in their own right, starting with cultivating collaborative cultures—a phenomenon that is as powerful as it is easy to get wrong.

Before proceeding, review Infographic 2 on Focusing Direction.

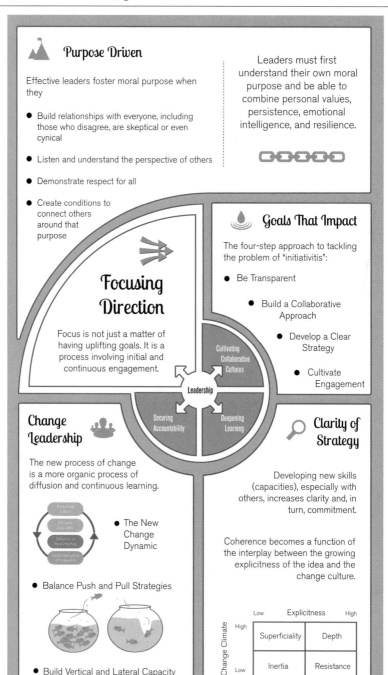

Purpose Driven

Effective leaders foster moral purpose when they

- Build relationships with everyone, including those who disagree, are skeptical or even cynical

- Listen and understand the perspective of others

- Demonstrate respect for all

- Create conditions to connect others around that purpose

Leaders must first understand their own moral purpose and be able to combine personal values, persistence, emotional intelligence, and resilience.

Focusing Direction

Focus is not just a matter of having uplifting goals. It is a process involving initial and continuous engagement.

Goals That Impact

The four-step approach to tackling the problem of "initiativitis":

- Be Transparent

- Build a Collaborative Approach

- Develop a Clear Strategy

- Cultivate Engagement

Leadership

Cultivating Collaborative Cultures

Securing Accountability

Deepening Learning

Change Leadership

The new process of change is a more organic process of diffusion and continuous learning.

- The New Change Dynamic

- Balance Push and Pull Strategies

- Build Vertical and Lateral Capacity and Integration

Clarity of Strategy

Developing new skills (capacities), especially with others, increases clarity and, in turn, commitment.

Coherence becomes a function of the interplay between the growing explicitness of the idea and the change culture.

	Explicitness	
	Low	High
High	Superficiality	Depth
Low	Inertia	Resistance

Change Climate

A full-color version of this infographic is also available for download at **http://www.corwin.com/books/Book244044** under "About" and then "Sample Materials and Chapters."

3

Cultivating Collaborative Cultures

> **Men Wanted**
>
> For hazardous journey, small wages, bitter cold, long months of complete darkness, constant danger, safe return doubtful, honor and recognition in case of success.
>
> —*Ernest Shackleton*

The fate of leaders today may not be quite so dire as described in Shackleton's alleged advertisement for his expedition to the South Pole, but the role is daunting nonetheless, as leaders need to engage and motivate others to collaborate on new solutions. The combination of rapid change, emerging technologies, and global complexity requires new processes for knowledge building. Charismatic heroes will not save the day. Rather, we need leaders who create a culture of growth; know how to engage the hearts and minds of everyone; and focus their collective intelligence, talent, and commitment to shaping a new path. They recognize that what pulls people in is meaningful work in collaboration with others. They *use the group to change the group* by building deep collaborative work horizontally and vertically across their organizations. They develop many leaders who, in turn, develop others, thereby contributing to the sustainability of the organization. It is this consistent, collective shaping and reshaping of ideas and solutions that forges deep coherence across the system.

Chapter 2 detailed the need to establish a focused direction that engages everyone with shared moral purpose, a small number of goals, a clear strategy for achieving them, and change leadership that mobilizes action. In this chapter, we examine the *driver of collaborative culture* as a dynamic force that uses relationships and shared expertise to turn complexities and fragmentation into a focused, coherent force for change. It's not about just creating a place where people feel good but rather about cultivating the expertise of everyone to be focused on a collective purpose. We have identified four elements of cultivating collaborative cultures: culture of growth, learning leadership, capacity building, and collaborative work (see Figure 3.1). Leaders who master these four elements will leverage collaborative culture within and across their organizations and build coherence for impact.

Figure 3.1   Cultivating Collaborative Cultures

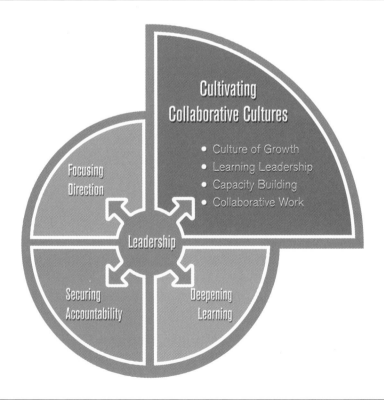

Note also that the nature of these collaborations is multifaceted. They focus on intraschool collaboration, increase schools–central office partnerships (see Johnson, Marietta, Higgins, Mapp, & Grossman, 2015), use lateral school-to-school networks within districts, and engage in district-to-district consortia and wider networks for teachers and educators.

Culture of Growth

Mind-set matters. Every action leaders take sends ripples through their organizations. The messages may be intended or unintended but can either build coherence and commitment or foster tension and frustration. Organizations that support learning, innovation, and action build a culture of growth. Leaders who possess a growth mind-set build capacity in others and help them achieve more than they expected of themselves. They see talent and potential and have strategies to unleash these qualities in others. Leaders who value a growth mind-set need to consider not just their words but also the messages they send as they pursue solutions to the challenges they face.

This mind-set of a culture of growth plays out in policy decisions and strategy. We consider two examples that convey strong messages to the organization—one that concerns leadership development and the other that focuses on planning. The first example centers on the policies and practices for developing leadership capacity. The stance a district takes in the development of its leaders has a strong impact on culture. Consider two popular TV shows as a metaphor and ask the following question: Is our organizational culture more like *Survivor* or *The Voice*? If you answered *Survivor,* the district likely selects leaders from a pool of volunteers; puts them through rigorous competition processes; places them in unfamiliar, hostile environments where competition and a win-at-all-costs mentality is fostered; and limits resources and trusting relationships. A negative culture of winners and losers emerges. Potential is overlooked, while individualistic and negative behaviors are reinforced.

Those who choose *The Voice* likely begin with volunteers but also cultivate those they feel have potential; use the selection process to enhance the natural talents of candidates by providing expert mentors, coaching, and resources (backup singers, lighting, etc.); and incorporate authentic performance tasks. The result is that skills are enhanced, confidence is increased, and a culture of collaboration emerges.

Let's translate this metaphor to districts and schools to consider how the culture of growth may be cultivated through the selection of leaders and teachers. When districts and schools believe that the solution will come from hiring external individuals, they send a message that the current staff is not up to the task. This creates a deficit culture that is apathetic at best, and demoralizing at worst, as everyone waits for someone to come in to save the day. We worked recently with a district that waited nine months for a principal they had hired from across the country to take up the post. In the interim, the school was stalled and the talent of the school leadership team was not realized. There were teacher-leaders inside the school who understood the dynamics, culture, and contexts of the staff and students. They had effective ideas about strategies to turn the school around but were kept in a holding pattern. This sent a strong message that "things are so bad here that only someone from 2,500 miles away can save the day and current staff are the problem, not part of the solution." This was a missed opportunity to build the collective talent, intelligence, and expertise to leverage collaborative culture.

When the organization values the talent and expertise of its people, it creates leadership development strategies that grow internal capacity. Its primary selection pool is drawn from within and augmented by external hires as needed. It creates a stream of successive development opportunities to grow leaders at all levels; selects them based on proven performance of authentic tasks; and provides ongoing coaching, mentoring, and development. It intentionally builds collaboration and learning for formal and informal leaders at all levels. In other words, collaborative cultures develop the next generation of leaders (as well as do better in the immediate term).

The same comparison can be made in the selection and development of teachers. Do we believe all teachers can perform at high levels, or are we trying to "fix" them with prepackaged program solutions? Do we rely on just hiring the best, or do we provide support for them to collaborate in meaningful ways? We know that doing work that has meaning is more motivating than any extrinsic rewards. People have an innate desire to belong and contribute—to be part of something bigger than themselves.

Our second example pertains to planning: using the example of the need to *develop a district plan for 21st century education*. All districts are grappling with the tension between implementing new standards and addressing emerging digital innovations. Consider two alternative district approaches for creating a plan and the impact of each approach on district culture:

- *District A* recognizes that the status quo will not allow them to sustain current levels of success, so they engage a prestigious consulting firm to recommend a plan. The firm audits their status through interviews with key groups within the district, interviews experts in the field, and prepares and presents to the board a 40-page blueprint for action.

- *District B* recognizes that the status quo will not allow them to sustain success so they select a task team of eight skilled principals plus four leaders from other levels of the district to form a task team. Their mandate is to provide a plan for moving the district forward. They are given *time* to engage in deep dialogue with each other and groups in the district; *resources* to connect with external experts and researchers; and the *opportunity* to visit external sites that have successful plans in action. They present a concise strategy for action.

Let's consider the impact of each strategy on three dimensions: quality of the plan, commitment to implement the plan, and capacity of the organization. District A's strategy sends messages to the organization that we don't think our people have the expertise to find solutions, we think the best ideas are outside our organization, and we need experts to translate them for us. As a result, their external strategy affects the organization in three important ways:

- The quality of the plan may be valued by the public and elected officials because of the firm's reputation but would likely not be as contextualized for internal audiences.

- Commitment to implementation would not be high since the shared meaning, ownership, and knowledge building reside with the external experts who did all the thinking and work.
- The capacity of the organization for solution finding for future issues would not be increased.

District B's approach sends clear messages to the organization that we value our people and their expertise as professionals, are committed to growing solutions internally while learning from the best ideas, and foster purposeful collaboration around meaningful work. As a result, their strategy impacts the organization in three important ways:

- The quality of the plan is enhanced because it is tailored to the context and culture.
- Commitment to implementation is already initiated during the solution-finding process and enhanced by the credibility of the local designers.
- The capacity of the organization to approach future issues is increased.

The lesson here is to seek good ideas externally, but don't rely on the external "experts" for solutions. Leaders at the school, district, and system levels are wise to evaluate policy and strategy decisions on the three dimensions of *quality, commitment,* and *capacity* to determine if the need for expediency is greater than the opportunity for growing the organization's capacity as well as the messages their approach will send. They should cultivate a rich dialogue both inside and outside the school, district, or state that informs the local solution finding.

Think about a major challenge you are facing in your organization and consider the following:

1. What is our current challenge?

2. What is our current capacity for solution finding?

3. Who has the greatest expertise or potential to address this either internally or externally?

4. How important is it to find a quick solution or to build the capacity of the organization to implement and find its own solutions?

5. What intended and unintended messages will our approach send to the organization?

We see a correlation between this growth mind-set culture and strong performance in student achievement in districts such as Long Beach, California; Fort Wayne Community Schools, Indiana; Garden Grove Unified School District, California; and York Region District School Board, Ontario, Canada. In each case, they have blended sustained capacity building with reliance on growing talent from within.

The old saying "actions speak so loudly no one can hear my words" is very apt. Consider the culture you espouse publicly and the policies and practices you have in place to determine if the intended and unintended messages are consistent. We turn next to the concept of lead learners who are essential in cultivating the growth mind-set and in building capacity across the organization.

Learning Leadership aka Lead Learners

Leaders at system, district, and school levels need to influence the culture and processes that support learning and working together in purposeful ways at every level of the organization if they are to produce greater learning in students. Creating a culture of growth is a start, but leaders need to intentionally orchestrate the work of teachers, leaders, and peers and keep it focused on collaboratively improving student learning.

In *The Principal* (Fullan, 2014c), I (Fullan) identified a major misstep that policy makers at state and district levels made in positioning the role of the principal as "instructional leader." They overinterpreted the research that the principal was the second (to the teacher) most important source of learning for students and proceeded to position the principal as conducting classroom visits, performing teacher appraisals, and taking corresponding action to develop or get rid of teachers who did not improve. We see at least some of these actions as valuable for the principal's own professional development in pedagogy but not as a way of moving the school. There are not enough hours in the week to micromanage teachers this way, and if one tries to do it diligently, it results in alienating principals and teachers from each other. Instead, principals have to become "lead learners," influencing teachers indirectly but nonetheless explicitly by helping to develop the group.

One powerful role for leaders centers on fostering professional capital (Hargreaves & Fullan, 2012). The professional capital framework has three components:

- *Human capital:* Refers to the human resource or personnel dimension of the quality of teachers—the basic skills and credentials. Attracting and developing these abilities of individuals is essential but not sufficient for impressive gains.
- *Social capital:* Encompasses the quality and quantity of interactions and relationships within the group. In schools, this affects teachers' access to knowledge and information; their sense of expectation, obligation, and trust; and their commitment to work together for a common purpose.
- *Decisional capital:* That which is required to make better decisions and results from the practical expertise across individuals and groups. When human and social capital are combined, decisional capital is enhanced.

Lead learners build professional capital across their organizations by *modeling learning, shaping culture,* and *maximizing the impact on learning.*

Modeling Learning

Robinson, Lloyd, and Rowe (2008) conducted research on the impact of school principals on student achievement and found that the most significant factor—twice as powerful as any other—was the degree to which the principal participated as a learner with staff in helping to move the school forward. Such principals model lead learning. They establish a culture where all teachers are expected to be continuous learners, and they lead the way. Lead learners who make the biggest impact don't send others to learn but actively participate with them as learning partners. In this way, principals learn what is specifically needed to stimulate ongoing organizational improvement. These principals make progress a collective endeavor—what we are calling collaborative work. Principals who do not take the "learner stance" for themselves do not keep ahead of the curve; they gain years of experience but not necessarily knowledge and skill about what is required to implement deeply. Principals who visibly struggle in learning about the Common Core State Standards (CCSS) or digital innovations along with teachers build credibility, trust, and knowledge of both the innovation and what is needed by the organization to move ahead. Most of all, *they learn,* thereby becoming more and more effective. Because they are immersed in action and tuned into learning, they recognize and mentor leadership in others. So, modeling is crucial for developing a learning culture.

Shaping Culture

A second key aspect involves shaping the culture to foster deeper relationships, trust, and engagement. Lead learners orchestrate structures and processes to create an environment that anticipates and works collaboratively on challenges and innovation. These principals don't spend their time on checklists and attempts to change teachers one teacher at a time but instead put their efforts into creating mechanisms of support and processes that build teacher collaboration, inquiry, and teams of leaders.

Research by Helen Timperley, in *Realizing the Power of Professional Learning* (2011), noted that "coherence across professional learning environments was not achieved through the completion of checklists and scripted lessons but rather through creating learning situations that promoted inquiry habits of mind throughout the school." Timperley offers the interesting metaphor for the principal "who is my class." With this filter, principals can identify the groups and individuals who can provide leadership for change. The principal's role becomes one of shaping the interactions and mechanisms while resourcing strategically those who propel collective learning. Lead learners support learning that is sustained and incorporate cycles of learning and application so that groups are learning from the work and engaging in solving authentic problems of implementation together.

Maximizing the Impact on Learning

Third, lead learners maximize the impact on student learning by relentlessly keeping the focus and conversation on quality learning for students and adults. They build precision by concentrating on a few goals and then developing a clear plan for achieving them. They build a collective understanding and engagement around the priorities so that every teacher and leader can answer, with equal ease and precision, the following questions: What are we doing? Why are we doing this?

The importance of lead learners—as modelers, culture shapers, and pressers for maximizing impact—was underscored in longitudinal research conducted in 477 elementary schools in Chicago (Bryk, Bender Sebring, Allensworth, Luppescu, & Easton, 2010). Bryk and colleagues found that 100 of the 477 schools had been able to make and sustain significant progress compared to their peers and that the key explanation was "school leadership as the driver for change." They noted four interrelated forces: the professional capacity of teachers, school climate, parent and community ties, and what they called the "instructional guidance system."

Lead learners are always monitoring impact but seldom rely on tools of performance appraisal, which are generally cumbersome and individualistic. Rather, they work on the instructional focus by orchestrating the work of coaches, teacher-leaders, and central office personnel to support student learning; focusing on the key elements; using data to diagnose learning needs; cultivating precision in instructional practices; and learning collectively. They facilitate processes that build collaborative inquiry into what works and what is needed to refine the approach. This cycle of learning simultaneously builds knowledge and skill, while reinforcing the culture of growth and collaborative improvement.

Capacity Building

Capacity building is a key lever for developing coherence because as knowledge and skills are being developed, the collaborative culture is deepened, shared meaning is clarified, and commitment is reinforced.

Capacity refers to the capability of the individual or organization to make the changes required and involves the development of knowledge, skills, and commitments. *Collective capacity building* involves the increased ability of educators at all levels of the system to make the instructional changes required to raise the bar and close the gap for all students.

Our experience was powerfully reinforced in the recent findings by John Hattie, building on Eells' (2011) work on "collective efficacy." Hattie's first books, *Visible Learning* (2009) and *Visible Learning for Teachers* (2012), identified that the highest instructional effect size on student learning was 1.44 (high expectations for each student). These findings came from an initial database of 800 meta studies. He has since added 400 or more studies, and the new winner is collective efficacy at 1.57 (although we should say that the depth of the knowledge base is not yet as established as with the other studies). As noted earlier, Hattie (2015) has now advanced this work under (what we would say is a more powerful concept) the idea of "collaborative expertise." The long and the short of all this is that the leader who helps develop focused collective capacity will make the greatest contribution to student learning.

Professional development does neither a great job on individual efficacy (learning wanes during implementation) nor collective efficacy. A huge gap exists between the promises of professional learning and results in student achievement. While professional learning materials, workshops, presenters, and programs abound, we often see a fragmented approach, focused on fixing individuals. Current programs solicit participation from individual schools and educators and often do not include systematic and sustained follow-up. The result is an overwhelming range of solutions without coherence or sustainability.

The key to a capacity building approach lies in developing a common knowledge and skill base across all leaders and educators in the system, focusing on a few goals, and sustaining an intense effort over multiple years. A capacity building approach creates a foundation for sustainable improvement as it does the following:

- Mobilizes a growth mind-set at all levels of the system
- Sustains and cultivates improved student learning
- Builds a common knowledge base and set of skills at all levels of the system

- Focuses on collaborative learning
- Emphasizes collective capacity, which engages everyone in the system with clear goals and commitment to the strategy for achievement
- Fosters cross-role learning or lateral capacity
- Incorporates a learning cycle of new learning, application on the job, reflection, and dialogue with colleagues

Capacity building is effective because it combines knowledge building, collective action, and consistent focus. When done well, it produces the following effects:

- Results in changed practices for leaders and in classrooms
- Provides a vehicle for learning from the work while doing the work
- Increases motivation and commitment because people have new skills and knowledge and see results sooner
- Engages more people in working on the new solutions
- Increases momentum and buy-in because people are part of a greater purpose
- Fosters leadership at all levels

Capacity building impacts the organization because it develops the culture; accelerates the speed of change; fosters sustainability; and reinforces the strategy as people become involved in deeper learning, reflection, and problem solving across the organization.

People sometimes have trouble grasping the concept of capacity building because it is more abstract than having a standard or making an assessment. Capacity building is an approach, not a program. The underlying concepts are consistent, but it can take different forms depending on the context. Here is a concrete example from our current work with districts. In partnership with the district, we form capacity building teams that learn within groups and across groups. We work with multiple levels of the system simultaneously. Typically, this includes learning strands for *district leaders, district capacity teams, principals,* and *school leadership teams.*

The approach at every level is to create communities of learners who develop common language, knowledge, skills, and commitment by building vertical and horizontal learning opportunities:

- District leaders form learning partnerships across roles and departments to develop a common language, knowledge base, and skills to focus on sustained development. They explore case examples and current research applied to their context. As a team, they refine the focus to a few key goals, sharpen the strategy, and rethink the resources and practices needed to achieve the goals.

- A district capacity team is composed of consultants or teacher-leaders who provide support to schools often by subject or project but often initially from a silo configuration. In a capacity building approach, all support providers form a learning community, and as they develop their common knowledge and strategy, they begin to interact in a more consistent manner so that innovations are not experienced by schools as a series of discrete initiatives but rather as an integrated, coherent strategy for change.

- Principals are the key to change. They work with peers as learning partners to build the skills needed to support capacity building at the school level.

- School leadership teams are composed of the principal and two to five teachers with a focus on improving learning and teaching. They are engaged as learning teams with other schools from the district to develop a common language, knowledge base, and set of skills to apply back in the school and classrooms. The cycle of learning approach has them implement the new understandings in their school and return to subsequent sessions to share their results and insights with other schools. This ensures that all participants understand deep learning communities by being a member of one. Teams develop short-term 60- to 100-day plans for cycles of inquiry and application to maximize moving to action and learning from it.

The formats and content vary depending on the district focus, but three features of the capacity building approach have demonstrated a strong impact in both changing practices and increasing coherence:

- Learning partnerships within teams and laterally across the organization
- Sustained focus over multiple sessions

- Cycles of learning from the work, which are structured inquiry with intentional application in roles and reflection on impact

The net effect is an increasing collective focus and corresponding capacities to learn together as well as make an impact on learning across the district.

Collaborative Work

Improving whole systems requires that everyone shift their practice. We saw in Chapter 2 that leaping from the current fishbowl to the new bowl of innovation requires new skills and knowledge (capacity building) but is accelerated when we combine it with deep collaborative work (finding other fish to learn and travel with on the journey). People are motivated to change through meaningful work done in collaboration with others. If we want to shift the organization, we need to pay attention to both the quality of the capacity building and the degree of collaborative learning. Figure 3.2 illustrates the relationship.

Figure 3.2 Shifting Organizational Practice

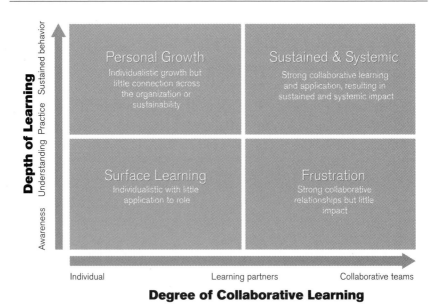

Depth of Learning

Depth of Learning, on the vertical axis of Figure 3.2, measures the quality of the learning design. It uses four stages of increasing quality: awareness, understanding, practice, and sustained behavior. When the design focuses on levels of awareness and understanding only, participants are passive learners, and research indicates that only about 15 percent of participants are able to put the new skill into practice. This makes sense because they have no experience with applying the new skill. High-quality learning designs also incorporate opportunities for participants to use the new skills or knowledge in safe environments and then in their roles and to get feedback from peers or coaches (practice). Adding the levels of application and coaching increases the likelihood that the behavior will be sustained as a regular practice by 90 percent or more of the participants (Joyce & Calhoun, 2010). This has tremendous implications for the allocation of resources when we can choose a 90 percent–plus return on investment or just 15 percent, depending on the strength of the learning design.

Degree of Collaborative Learning

The horizontal axis measures the degree of collaborative work or learning together. It is described as a continuum from completely individual through a range of learning partnerships to integrated collaborative work. Hattie's finding of a 1.57 impact for collective efficacy suggests that the horizontal axis can be a significant accelerator when done well.

Four combinations of quality of the learning design and degree of collaboration are described next:

- *Surface learning:* Occurs when the experience is very individualized and the depth of the intervention is weak—predominantly telling, finding, or modeling. This may result from one-shot workshops and random accessing of online resources without a linkage to broader goals or application. The result is surface learning with limited shift in sustainable behavior.
- *Personal growth:* Occurs when the experience is individualized but the learning design is strong and includes opportunity for feedback

and application over time. The quadrant does not mean that individual learning is bad and collaborative is always good, but that individual learning can be weak when it is random, fragmented, and has little opportunity for feedback or application. Individual learning, with a strong learning design, can be highly effective when it is focused, provides feedback, and has opportunities for application in the role.

- *Frustration:* Occurs when people are putting a lot of effort into learning together, such as professional learning communities (PLCs) or networks, but the experience is not well designed or executed. There may be little or no opportunity to apply the learning in real situations with feedback or time is spent in a series of tasks or topics with little follow-up or application.
- *Sustained and systemic shifts:* Occur when there are strong collaborative work structures combined with good learning design. Learning is sustained and explored in depth with opportunities for application within roles. Coaches, mentors, and peers stimulate learning and provide timely feedback. Examples include focused use of collaborative inquiry models, institutes, learning labs, and work-based learning teams.

If one wants to shift school, district, or system practices, one needs to have a strong learning design *and* deeper collaborative work. Take, for example, implementation of the CCSS. When the learning design is limited to "unpacking" the standards and comparing them to previous standards, teachers have no opportunity to develop the new skills that will be needed to teach the new standards. Whether they work individually or in collaboration, the design is weak and the ability to make a difference for student learning is limited (what we call surface learning or frustration).

If, however, we have collaborative teams using the new standards to design learning for their students, teaching using the standards and the newly designed learning, and then reflecting with peers on the student work and observations resulting from the new approach, we begin to see real shifts in practice over a short period of time. Repeating cycles of collaborative design, teaching, and reflection is a powerful way to build understanding, skill, and commitment, moving the approach toward systemic and sustained.

When quality learning design and collaborative work combine, individuals learn new skills and build knowledge while the meaningful collaborative work deepens and refines their practice by giving opportunities for dialogue and feedback. This, in turn, reinforces and shapes the shared purpose and builds ownership. Shifting practice in organizations takes time, focus, and persistence. Facilitating strong collaborative work processes and structures is an example of using the group to change the group and greatly increases the likelihood of persistence until sustained and systemic shifts become part of "the way we do things around here."

We have stated that collaborative work can be a powerful accelerator of change and learning, but not all collaborative work approaches are effective. The popularity of the concept of PLCs has been far greater than its consistent impact on student learning (see DuFour & Fullan, 2013).

A recent publication by the Boston Consulting Group (BCG), commissioned by the Gates Foundation, found that while PLCs are prevalent, teachers "are not satisfied with implementation to date" (BCG, 2014, p. 5). The good news in the study is that districts are recognizing the need to shift from one-shot workshops to more robust approaches, such as lesson study, coaching, and PLCs. The troubling news is that the implementation is weak. The most common form of professional learning is still workshops. While we see increasing examples of coaching, fewer than 50 percent of teachers had experienced a deep level of coaching in the last few months, and coaching time seems to be directed toward new and struggling teachers. The proliferation of PLCs has often evolved with the philosophy of let 1,000 flowers bloom. We see blocks of dedicated PLC time established across schools and districts that is often no more than time in search of a purpose or spent on a multitude of tasks that do not directly result in improved learning for students. We see teams spending countless hours analyzing data but seldom spending the same amount of time in designing more precise pedagogy to meet the identified needs.

The concept of learning communities is not wrong, but the implementation has lacked depth. If we embrace the idea that our students should be critical thinkers grounded in metacognition, then we need to design learning experiences for adults that foster the same competencies because *we cannot give to others what we do not possess ourselves.* If we want our systems to be authentic—energizing environments for students—then we must create them for the adults as well. Deep collaborative experiences that are tied to daily work, spent designing and assessing learning, and built on teacher choice and input can dramatically energize teachers and increase results.

In short, effective collaborative work has key attributes that must be attended to.

We use the term *collaborative work* to connote deeper experiences that have the power to affect student learning. Collaborative work approaches must be intentionally designed and implemented to do the following:

- Incorporate whole systems so that everyone is learning.
- Focus on learning and pedagogical improvement.
- Build capacity to support implementation and innovation.
- Have a measurable impact with specific goals and indicators.
- Be flexible and dynamic to meet emerging needs.
- Be sustainable.

Meaningful collaborative work is more likely to flourish when the foundational conditions are in place. Essentially, these conditions are the four components of the Coherence Framework: focus and purpose, collaboration underpinned with specific capacities, deep learning, and internal accountability.

Collaborative Work in Action

The shift toward deeper forms of connected learning is emerging at every level of our organizations. Here, we explore promising approaches at the state, province, district, and school levels, including collaborative inquiry; networks and collaboratives; and personal learning networks (PLNs) leveraging technology and social media. What is common about these strategies is that they involve the group, have focused goals, develop capacity, seek precision of pedagogical practice, link the work to measurable impacts on student learning, and are well led for these very purposes.

Collaborative Inquiry

Ontario Focused Intervention Partnership

The Teaching-Learning Critical Pathway (TLCP) is a promising model used to organize actions for teaching and student learning. The basic idea of the pathway is that when classroom practice is examined collaboratively, it leads to increased student achievement for all. The Ontario approach is based on collaborative inquiry that involves new ways of working together (Ontario Ministry of Education, 2007b).

In Ontario, the critical learning instructional path was adapted and used with over 800 low-performing schools to provide targeted, nonpunitive, and transparent support called the Ontario Focused Intervention Partnership (OFIP). The results were dramatic, with fewer than 100 schools designated as poor performing after three years of use.

The process involves four key steps (see Figure 3.3):

Figure 3.3   Collaborative Inquiry: Four Key Steps

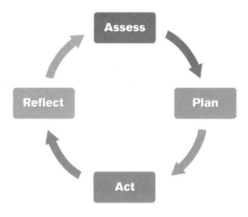

Assess: A group of teachers, usually a grade team, gathers evidence of current student achievement to identify areas of need. They identify curriculum standards related to that need and review current instructional practices. Together, they design a common assessment that will be administered at the conclusion of the six-week learning cycle.

Plan: The team develops a six-week learning block based on the standards and selects high-yield instructional strategies. If needed, they engage in professional learning targeted to the identified needs.

Act: The team implements the learning design in their classrooms. Teachers select students to watch as "markers" and will share their progress with the grade team. Teachers monitor both the appropriateness of the instruction and the progress of students. They provide scaffolding and adjustments as needed over the six weeks. They administer the common assessment as a culminating task and collect samples of student work.

Reflect: In the final stage, the team conducts a teacher moderation cycle using the collected samples of work. Teachers collaboratively assess student work for the "marker" students and identify next steps needed in the student learning. These strategies can usually be applied to groups of students. Next, the team engages in reflection to determine the effectiveness of the learning design and the high-yield strategies chosen and the next steps needed to deepen learning. Ways to support students who were not yet successful are identified, and the data on the learning design and student learning feed into the next six-week cycle.

The power of this model has been to focus transparently on a clear target in a way that motivates and builds capacity across the school. The provincial support included training in the processes and facilitation and fostered a sense of partnership to achieve a common goal of increased student achievement. Teachers, superintendents, and teacher-leaders describe the process as highly challenging but also as the best professional experience they have had. This version of collaborative inquiry merges the best features of lesson study and examination of student work. It ensures that both the learning and teaching are thoughtfully designed and assessed and moves the conversation from simply analyzing data to robust discussion of ways to shift instruction to improve student learning.

This deep collaborative work requires new ways of working together, trust, shared leadership, sustained focus, and a commitment to collaborative inquiry. It works because reflection and collaborative examination of practice become part of the culture of the school and district. While the intervention was first piloted with underperforming schools, word spread quickly that it was having a strong impact on student learning. Other schools began asking for the capacity building in facilitation skills, and it has now become a widespread practice across the 4,000 schools in Ontario, thus increasing coherence at both the school and district levels.

Improvement Science

Anthony Bryk, president of the Carnegie Foundation for the Advancement of Teaching, proposes using improvement science to accelerate learning and address problems of practice because "we need smarter systems, organizations capable of learning and improving, that see learning and change as what it means to be vital, to be alive" (Bryk, Gomez, Grunow, & Le Mahieu, 2014). Bryk et al. (2014) set out "six principles of improvement." The authors describe improvement science as explicitly designed to accelerate learning-by-doing, utilizing a user-centered and problem-centered approach to improving teaching and learning. The overall goal is to develop the necessary *know-how* for a reform idea to spread faster and more effectively. A key component of their approach is a structure called networked improvement communities (NICs).

NICs are intentionally designed social organizations, each with a distinct problem-solving focus. These structured networks have norms of practice, roles, and responsibilities. NICs are scientific communities because they are focused on a well-specified common aim guided by a deep understanding of the problem, the system that produces it, and a shared working theory to improve it; disciplined by the methods of improvement research to develop, test, and refine interventions; organized to accelerate interventions into the field; and designed to effectively integrate them into varied educational contexts.

These communities use a 90-day cycle (Park & Takahashi, 2013), which includes three phases:

- *Scan:* The team reviews pertinent current and academic knowledge on the topic, then narrows to a specific issue and identifies a product or framework to be tested for 30 days.
- *Focus:* The participants use rapid, small-scale testing to assess the prototype or framework over 30 days.
- *Summarize:* The team refines its innovation and summarizes its work in a 90-day cycle report including what the cycle has produced.

At the conclusion of the cycle, a decision is made on how to use or share the findings. This improvement approach is a powerful way to bring precision to collaborative work as it incorporates rigor in the examination of the issue and requires an outcome based on authentic application and reflection.

Networks

Networks are proliferating in a variety of formats and attract both individuals and groups. Results can be dramatic or mediocre, depending on the design elements. Interest in collaborating across districts is evolving rapidly. Currently, we are working with 10 (mostly large) school districts in California, serving more than one million students. The districts have created vertical leadership teams representing levels within the district and are engaged in multiyear collaborative learning focused on rethinking, leadership, and increased coherence. In another project, we are working with three districts in California over a three-year period. Across the country, we are working with a cohort of 28 school districts in Connecticut on leadership to maximize coherence. This effort is supported by five professional organizations that are bringing vertical teams together to engage in cycles of learning and engagement in a multiyear experience. These are just three of many examples of districts that are seeing the value of deep collaborative work that engages new ideas and applies them in context. We next share two examples that are intentionally organized to shift practice in organizations across and within districts.

System Transformation Collaborative

Three school districts in Northern California—Pittsburg Unified, San Lorenzo Unified, and Napa Valley Unified—are engaged in a three-year *collaborative* with us, focused on sustainable system improvement and enhanced cross-school and cross-district collaboration.

The three district leadership teams attend joint learning sessions quarterly to increase their skills as change leaders, develop clarity about system goals and strategy, and enhance collaborative cultures. Between sessions, they apply the new learning in their roles and return to share evidence of impact. This is an example of using the group to change the group as the peer connections across districts both raise the bar and stimulate new thinking about common issues.

School leadership teams composed of principals and three to eight teachers attend quarterly sessions to deepen instructional coherence and improve student learning. They engage in within-school and cross-school examination of cases and simulations during the sessions and design 60-day learning cycles to apply the new ideas in their schools. They return to subsequent sessions to share evidence of impact on other staff and student learning. The collaborative learning cycle is a key lever for inquiry into practices that work in the local context.

After 18 months, participants describe the impact in three areas: they are developing a common language and knowledge base across the districts, the design is building both vertical and lateral capacity, and they articulate and act with greater clarity of focus and strategy. Patrick Sweeney, superintendent of Napa, stated recently, "We are getting traction now." Teachers and principals talk about the way the new skills and knowledge are helping them navigate the implementation of the CCSS and new assessments by providing a focus on quality learning for both the adults and the students. Learning fairs are held each year for schools and districts to reflect on the achievements and insights gleaned from the work and to collate evidence of impact.

This *system transformation collaborative* is building coherence and impact because it increases clarity of goals and strategy; provides sustained learning experiences with cycles of application and reflection; increases both vertical and lateral capacity building; and fosters relentless focus on student learning.

Ontario Networked Learning Community

Across the province of Ontario, examples of networked learning communities for teachers and school leaders are on the rise. Groups form with a specific purpose, establish norms, and use protocols to keep focused. Using a collaborative inquiry model, they access research, examine questions, serve as critical friends, and focus on ways to use best practice as well as to learn new practices. A question format promotes thoughtful reflection and encourages team members to dig deeply into the *why* of the inquiry.

A recent report on effective learning teams and networks with school leaders (Leskiw-Janvary, Oakes, & Waler, 2013) identified six key factors that increased the impact of these networks:

- *Collaborative inquiry:* Collective learning and understanding encourages innovation and meaning while practices are analyzed, leading to purposeful, effective action.
- *Leadership:* All members share flexible, emergent leadership by asking effective, timely questions to create the compelling disturbances that generate new ideas and questions.

- *Relationships:* All members take risks within a trusting environment and operate in interdependent ways.
- *Instructional focus:* A continuous process with evidence of new, quality thinking and intentional changes in practice is embedded. Groups are established based on explicit needs, and meaningful, relevant, appropriate data are strategically collected.
- *Reflection:* Ongoing focused reflection leads to integration of learning and deeper understanding. Theories of action are refined based on new learning that results in a change in practice.
- *Accountability:* As a result of collective learning, changes in teacher instructional practice lead to improved student outcomes.

School leaders in the networks point out that they always begin with the needs of the school. Trust and relationships are key, and they note that the variety of experience levels in the network means they learn with one another and on behalf of one another. They see this as building capacity that is leading to sustainability across the district and the province.

Harnessing the Power of Personal Learning Networks 2.0

A new form of collaborative interaction is spreading through social networking, online communities, and collaboration platforms. Early use has been somewhat random, with varied levels of engagement and impact, but our *lean start-up* philosophy suggests that future iterations will be increasingly more powerful if we harness the power of virtual connections and connect it to focused purpose.

Two forces are combining to propel the use of virtual networks: time and global reach. Educators feel universally overwhelmed with demands on their time, and virtual connections allow them freedom to connect anytime, anywhere to share learning designs, strategies, and collaboration across grades, departments, or schools. Second, virtual tools allow users to connect with leaders and teachers from anywhere who may be working on common interests or give new perspectives to the work.

Formats for connection are expanding rapidly from e-mail and Twitter to blogs, social bookmarking, groups, forums, and collaborative platforms. One downside for users is finding a way to keep track of the deluge of information and to avoid the distraction of interesting but not necessarily relevant information.

We highlight one attempt at a state level to utilize the power of technology and virtual networks to address core issues.

The New Hampshire Network Strategy

New Hampshire wanted a system that would fundamentally change how they support districts with a goal of moving from a compliance-oriented culture to one of greater support that better serves the needs of students. Their strategy is founded on a belief in the power of networks to promote change and deepen adult learning, and that success will be defined by moving students to true college and career readiness. This requires the building of capacity of educators as they note the following:

> The strategy's focus is to build and support relationships by connecting educators and districts across our state to one another, to high quality information resources and professional learning supports, as well as to promote greater alignment between and among statewide initiatives. (New Hampshire Department of Education, 2013, p. 4)

The strategy comprises two features: *professional learning networks* based on district needs and state goals, and the New Hampshire Network Platform, which is a virtual space for educators to collaborate and learn.

The design began by understanding district needs, which ranged from implementation of CCSS to use of data by school-based teams. The identified needs were used to establish learning objectives for the professional learning networks. Launched in November 2012, over 1,800 educators participated in workshops, conferences, and webinars in the first seven months.

As they continue to refine the strategy, they plan to capture broader evidence of impact, but comments from participants are positive.

> We are engaging many more people now. . . . We are casting a broader net, which is probably the largest change, in terms of district growth. Instead of picking the five or ten all star teachers we have a lot of people who are aware and encourage others. (New

Hampshire Department of Education, 2013, p. 24) (referring to the Gilford School District)

"Coming together with other cohorts and with fidelity and in a collaborative fashion so people own it has not been the practice," but the network strategy helps propel us in that direction. "More and more we are looking at community and looking forward." (New Hampshire Department of Education, 2013, p. 26) (referring to the Keen School District [SAU29], p. 26)

The change strategy incorporated a prototyping for the first six months and then revisions based on early data. Four lessons emerged:

Lesson One: This is complex work. Shifting from compliance to capacity support is challenging. They noted a tension between balancing the requirements of being a regulatory body and what is needed to support transformation in and meet current expectations of users for support.

Lesson Two: Clear communication is key. Designers needed to be clearer about goals and connections as well as integrating the components of the strategy into a stronger whole.

Lesson Three: Formalize the structure. While participants reported a good experience, feedback revealed areas for refinement and greater timeliness in providing options.

Lesson Four: Changing behaviors takes time. Technology was not the driver of collaboration or problem solving—that requires a shift in changing perceptions and actions from within the New Hampshire Department of Education as well as in districts, which means shifting from a focus on the initiative to cultivating relationships.

New Hampshire's end game is to grow a marketplace where high-quality professional learning supports are offered and to shift the relationships from compliance to support. We see promise in this effort as it has avoided the simple allure of technology as a panacea and has focused on building relationships and two-way communication. Their design incorporates rapid prototyping informed by feedback cycles from the field; combining virtual connection with focused, meaningful purpose and protocols to maximize involvement and depth of learning; and recognizing that coherence will only emerge from an integrated effort. We look forward to seeing the results of this combination.

Final Thoughts

Collaborative work is a key driver in shifting behavior. It is the social glue that moves the organization toward coherence. We see from the previously given examples that there is no one way to build a culture of growth or to learn collaboratively, but every success works on the same focused collaborative agenda relative to system goals.

The reflections of astronaut Chris Hadfield, as he built his photography skills to capture images of Earth while orbiting in space, capture the essence of the learning journey leaders must take.

> Every chance we have we float over to see what's changed since we last went around the earth. There's always something new to see because the planet itself is rotating, so each orbit takes us over different parts of it. . . . Over time, my ability to understand what I was seeing improved. I started to look forward to certain places and lighting conditions, in the way you love to hear a piece of music. . . . I became more adept at noticing and interpreting the secrets Earth was discretely revealing. My ability to photograph what I was seeing also improved. I started to figure out how to compose a shot in a way that draws attention to particular features and textures. (Hadfield, 2014)

As leaders, we must hone our skills in recognizing the *particular features and textures* of our contexts, noting the nuances of building relationships, and engaging others in this challenging work. These developments are especially critical as we experience the rapid change of what we call "the Stratosphere agenda" (Fullan, 2013c). Traditional schooling is increasingly generating bored and alienated students and teachers. The allure of digital and better engaging pedagogy is combining to disrupt existing classrooms. There was never a time when collaborative power was more needed to work through absolutely rapid change dynamics aimed at deep learning (see Chapter 4). Only the purposefully collaborative will survive!

Collaborating is turning out to be a powerful but complex strategy. There is a whole body of research that indicates that much—indeed, we would say most—collaboration is problematic. Sunstein and Hastie (2015), in their book *Wiser,* devote the first five chapters to "How Groups Fail": individuals go along with the crowd (groupthink), groups amplify errors, they take polarized positions, and so on. In another publication, *Freedom to Change,* Fullan (2015) makes the case that it is essential that individuals maintain *both* their autonomy and their collaboration.

But for our purposes, we are on safe ground with our Coherence Framework.

Within the collaborating component in this chapter, we showed that collaborating must include four key ingredients: the need to build a culture of growth through not only our words but our actions; the role that lead learners play to model, shape, and maximize learning for all; strategies for capacity building; and approaches for fostering deep collaborative work. Leaders who are able to combine these four elements build a culture horizontally and vertically across their organizations that is resilient because purpose and meaning are internalized, sustainable because it is owned and coherent because they are working on it day in day out, and it becomes the way "we do things around here."

We also stress that the four components of our model serve as cross-cutting reinforcements. For example, collaborating—this chapter—plays itself out in relation to focused direction, deep learning, and securing accountability. These inherent checks and balances increase the integrity of the model as a whole. As part of understanding the full model, it's time to go deeper into learning.

Before turning to Chapter 4, review Cultivating Collaborative Cultures in Infographic 3.

Culture of Growth

Organizations that support learning, innovation, and action build a culture of growth.

Mind-set matters.

Seek good ideas externally, but don't rely on the external experts for solutions.

Leaders are wise to evaluate policy and strategy decisions on the three dimensions of quality, commitment, and capacity.

Learning Leadership

Lead learners build professional capital across their organizations by

Modeling learning

Shaping the culture

Maximizing the focus on learning

Cultivating Collaborative Cultures

Collaborating is not just about creating a place where people feel good but rather about cultivating the expertise of everyone to be focused on a collective purpose.

Capacity Building

Effective change processes shape and reshape good ideas as they build capacity and ownership.

- -

The key to a capacity building approach lies in

- Developing a common knowledge and skill base across all leaders and educators in the system

- Focusing on a few goals

- Sustaining an intense effort over multiple years

Capacity building is an approach, not a program.

Focusing Direction

Leadership

Securing Accountability

Deepening Learning

Collaborative Work

To shift school, district, or system practices, one needs to have a strong learning design and deep collaborative work.

Collaborative work approaches must be intentionally designed and implemented to

- Incorporate whole systems
- Focus on learning
- Build capacity
- Have measurable impact
- Be flexible and dynamic
- Be sustainable

 A full-color version of this infographic is also available for download at **http://www.corwin.com/ books/Book244044** under "About" and then "Sample Materials and Chapters."

4

··

Deepening
Learning

··

Once in a while there is a convergence of independent but relatable forces that come together and create synergetic breakthroughs in societal learning. We are at the early stages of a potentially powerful confluence of factors that could transform education.

—Michael Fullan (2013c)

There is a learning revolution under way because of the confluence of forces. These forces are urgency, knowledge, and capacity. The urgency evolves from the allure of a dynamic, fast-paced, multimedia global world competing with traditional schooling that has not changed much in 50 years. Schooling as we have known it is outdated. This creates a push-pull dynamic. The push factor is that schools are increasingly boring for students and alienating for teachers. A recent Gallup poll (2014) found only 53 percent of students are engaged. Other studies show even less of a connection to schools on the part of students such as Jenkins (2013), who finds that by the time students reach grade 9 less than 40 percent of students are enthusiastic about being in school (see also Quaglia & Corso, 2014). This lack of engagement by at least half of students polled is translating into underperformance and ultimately a lack of preparedness for life as Gallup also found that high scores in the engagement index resulted in strong achievement gains. The pull factor is that innovations in the digital world are alluring, omnipresent, and accessible outside the walls of the school (alluring but not yet necessarily productive).

A second force for change is the emerging knowledge base in both pedagogy and change leadership. Cognitive science and research on learning, such as John Hattie's *Visible Learning for Teachers* (2012), has given us the tools to make learning effective. At the same time, we have insights into ways to use digital to accelerate learning. In short, pedagogy and digital are intersecting to open radical new ways of engagement and deeper learning.

When we link the new knowledge about pedagogy and digital to "change knowledge"—knowledge about how to mobilize individuals and groups as they innovate—we will get breakthroughs in how learning occurs. We call this "the Stratosphere agenda" (Fullan, 2013c). Imagine a school where all of the students are so excited that they can't wait to get there and want to carry on their learning at the end of the school day. Students are connecting with each other and experts across the globe as they research, solve problems, collaborate, and connect with their communities. Imagine the excitement of creating their own solar energy source or developing a campaign to end hunger in their community. Students are not only building the foundational literacy and content expertise but also, more importantly, learning to learn. Discipline problems disappear because students are so engaged, and learning becomes a 24/7 endeavor. Parents demonstrate their support by contributing to the learning at home and virtually. This may sound utopian, but we see glimmers of this type of innovation in classrooms, schools, and districts where they are transforming learning for both students and adults alike. The innovations show promise, but they are often isolated examples.

So why isn't better learning happening everywhere? It's not because of the inputs. Ask any grandparent of a three-year-old, and they will assure you that they are geniuses—full of curiosity, persistence, and creativity. However, by the age of eight, we begin to see the signs of apathy and boredom setting in, and this escalates throughout the high school years. Traditional schooling has become disconnected from the life of students outside of school—from the real world. And the boredom is not restricted to the students, as we heard from a principal in an innovative school: "Teachers were bored too; they just didn't know it." These are strong *push* factors for change. At the same time, the world of digital learning, gaming, and connectivity is exploding as a pull factor that is irresistible but often too random to be productive.

This brings us to the third force of capacity. How, then, do we mobilize the energy of this push-pull dynamic to innovate in a sustainable way? No system or district in the world has made significant gains for students without a relentless focus on the learning and teaching process. The challenge is to move from isolated innovations in some classrooms or some schools to transformation for every classroom, school, district, and beyond.

Two notions are critical. First, we must shift from a focus on teaching or inputs to a deeper understanding of the process of *learning* and how we can influence it. The past two decades of preoccupation with high-stakes testing resulted in fragmentation of the learning process into small bits of content and skills that were practiced in rote styles. The recent introduction of the Common Core State Standards (CCSS) holds the promise of a shift to learning that is more authentic, rigorous, and meaningful. That promise will only be fulfilled if we can engender a new partnership for learning in our schools and classrooms that is built on precision in the new pedagogies. Second, *relentless focus* (or "focused direction") means we must abandon the notion that there is a silver bullet, package, or program (including technology) that is a solution and recognize that the next shift in learning will require knowledge building by everyone engaged and must affect *all* students. We can shape how children connect with the world and with each other and create deep learners who are curious and committed. The choice is ours, but time is running out because our kids can't wait; they won't wait.

We have already established that persistent focused direction and innovation is foundational (Chapter 2) and that purposeful collaborating is the pathway to progress (Chapter 3). Unless that focus and collaboration are directed to the improvement of the learning-teaching process, we are likely to see a lot of activity with little impact on students. This *deepening learning* is our third component of the Coherence Framework. Let's now turn to how systems can dramatically improve engagement by using the right driver of deepening learning. There are three elements that deepen learning by doing the following (see Figure 4.1):

1. Establish clarity of deep learning goals.

2. Build precision in pedagogies accelerated by digital.

3. Shift practices through capacity building.

Figure 4.1 Deepening Learning

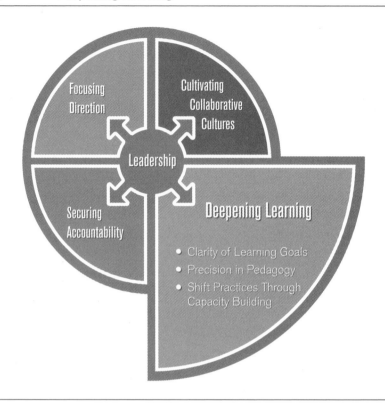

Schools, districts, and systems that mobilize the right driver of deepening learning will cultivate clarity of learning outcomes, identify and shape the new pedagogies combined with digital innovations to build precision, and use collaborative learning to shift practices. Many districts and schools are already overwhelmed with poverty, poor performance, and multiple mandates as well as trying to get the basics in place. How do they address this shift to the digital and global worlds? The solution lies in becoming both learners and reflective doers who are working on continuous improvement and innovation simultaneously. It means going deeper in improving the foundations such as literacy and mathematics while engaging in focused innovation on developing what we call *deep learning competencies*.

Leaders at the district, state, and school levels need to ask this question: What are the two or three things that will most improve student learning? These may be better strategies for the foundational literacy skills or new learning partnerships that use technology to accelerate learning. In all cases, it is essential to build clarity of the learning goals, build precision in the pedagogical practices, and to foster collective capacity building to mobilize a consistent shift in practices.

Before taking up the three elements of deepening learning, we should revisit the role of technology or digital. We have cast technology as a wrong driver—not because it is always wrong but because without precise pedagogy it is ineffective. This is why researchers like John Hattie and Larry Cuban unequivocally find that the use of technology has a negligible impact on learning. The reason is that technology by and large has been used superficially or poorly pedagogically, not because it has no potential. This remains the case today—that is, the predominant strategy is still based on "acquisition." The past 30 years have seen billions poured into the acquisition of digital devices and software, with few whole system gains in student performance to show for it. The single implementation strategy of acquisition has given limited attention to developing the new pedagogies that would use technology as an accelerator, or the capacity building essential to ensure educators had the skill and knowledge to use technology to amplify learning. This is changing, and we are part of that shift in practice in our New Pedagogies for Deep Learning (NPDL) initiative (www.NPDL.global). In this new model, pedagogy is the driver and digital is the accelerator to go faster and deeper into learning for all.

Across the globe and in every facet of life, we are seeing three trends that are combining to shift educators from simply acquiring technology to using the right driver of *pedagogy accelerated by digital*: the proliferation of digital into every facet of living, the impact of globalization, and the emerging new pedagogies for learning.

In *The New Digital Age: Reshaping the Future of People, Nations and Business,* authors Eric Schmidt and Jared Cohen (2013) offer insights into how the digital world and globalization are combining to force change:

> Soon everyone on earth will be connected. With 5 billion more people set to join the virtual world, the boom in digital connectivity will bring gains in productivity, health, education, quality of life and myriad other avenues in the physical world—and this will

be true for everyone, from the most elite users to those at the base of the economic pyramid.

New levels of collaboration and cross pollination across different sectors internationally will ensure that many of the best ideas and solutions will have a chance to rise to the top and be seen, considered, explored, funded, adopted and celebrated. (p. 1)

They predict that the most important pillar behind innovation and opportunity is education and that tremendous positive change will occur as rising connectivity reshapes traditional routines and offers new paths for learning. They identify five ways the Internet is propelling the new digital age:

- The Internet has transformed itself from simple information transmission into an endlessly multifaceted outlet for human energy and expression.
- Never before in history have so many people, from so many places, had so much power at their fingertips.
- The proliferation of communication technologies has advanced at an unprecedented speed and is spreading to the farthest reaches of the planet, at an accelerating rate.
- By 2015, the majority of the world's population will, in one generation, have gone from having virtually no access to unfiltered information to processing all of the world's information through a device that fits in the palm of the hand.
- The form of connectivity doubles roughly every nine months. . . . The promise of exponential growth unleashes possibilities in graphics and virtual reality that will make the online experience as real as real life, or perhaps even better. (Schmidt & Cohen, 2013)

Technology and global-driven change is inevitable, but we have a choice in how we prepare our next generation for that challenge. We can choose to focus on learning and use pedagogy as the driver and technology as the accelerator. This involves engaging in rapid cycles of innovation, learning from the work, and improving with each iteration.

As usual, we pursue these new developments by partnering with practitioners. The best way to break new ground is to get to action around a stimulating agenda. Our biggest foray is NPDL. We plan to partner with approximately 10 clusters of on the average 100 schools in 10 countries (1,000 schools) to learn together through the following:

1. New partnerships between and among students, teachers, and families

2. New pedagogical practices linked to 21st century learning outcomes (what we call the 6Cs—communication, critical thinking, collaboration, creativity, character, and citizenship)

3. Change leadership at the school and system levels. So far, we are working with eight countries and over 500 schools.

We are also aware that in addition to the New Pedagogies Partnership and CCSS, countless other schools and districts, some of which we work with, are engaged in similar agendas. They will need to sort out the three elements within our deep learning component of the Coherence Framework: (1) clarity of learning goals, (2) precision in pedagogy, and (3) shifting practice.

Develop Clarity of Learning Goals

The first step in building precision and consistent practices is to be clear about the learning goals. For the last quarter century, education has been giving superficial lip service to 21st century skills without much concerted action or impact. The energy has been invested in describing sets of skills without much robust implementation or effective ways to measure them. If we want to mobilize concerted action and a deep shift in practice then governments, districts, and schools need to develop clarity of outcomes and build shared understanding of these by educators, students, and parents. The CCSS is a step in the direction of deeper learning.

NPDL is developing clarity of learning goals for what it calls deep learning. Deep learning involves using new knowledge to solve real-life problems and incorporates a range of skills and attributes. The global partnership is working to define with specificity six deep learning competencies (the 6Cs), describe what the learning would look like for each of these, identify the pedagogies that foster those competencies, and design new measures to assess student progress in developing them. Their deep learning competency framework and initial descriptors of each competency and its dimensions are displayed in Figure 4.2.

Figure 4.2   Deep Learning Competencies—The 6Cs

Communication

- Coherent communication using a range of modes
- Communication designed for different audiences
- Substantive, multimodal communication
- Reflection on and use of the process of learning to improve communication

Critical Thinking

- Evaluating information and arguments
- Making connections and identifying patterns
- Problem solving
- Meaningful knowledge construction
- Experimenting, reflecting, and taking action on ideas in the real world

Collaboration

- Working interdependently as a team
- Interpersonal and team-related skills
- Social, emotional, and intercultural skills
- Management of team dynamics and challenges

Creativity

- Economic and social entrepreneurialism
- Asking the right inquiry questions
- Considering and pursuing novel ideas and solutions
- Leadership for action

Character

- Learning to learn
- Grit, tenacity, perseverance, and resilience
- Self-regulation and responsibility
- Empathy for and contributing to the safety and benefit of others

Citizenship

- A global perspective
- Understanding of diverse values and worldviews
- Genuine interest in human and environmental sustainability
- Solving ambiguous, complex, and authentic problems

Source: NPDL (2014).

The overall purpose of the 6Cs is the well-being of the whole student but also the well-being of the group and society as a whole. Learning becomes the development of competencies for the successful negotiation of an uncertain world. Learning is about developing the personal and interpersonal and cognitive capabilities that allow one to diagnose what is going on in the complex, constantly shifting human and technical context of real-world practice and then match an appropriate response (Fullan & Scott, 2014).

This new conceptualization of what we need to be successful in life is gaining attention in all sectors. In her book *Thrive* (2014), Ariana Huffington describes how as CEO and cofounder of the Huffington Post Media Group, she almost worked herself into a grave by the age of 40. She collapsed from exhaustion after two years of 18-hour days, seven days a week. She recalibrated her life and determined that in addition to money and power, there is a third metric that consists of a syndrome that includes the following: well-being, wisdom, wonder, and giving. She discovered new core values, and we must help students develop a keen sense of what they value and are committed to being and doing.

In this context, Fullan and Scott (2014) suggest that well-being and success in life incorporate two big Es: *entrepreneurialism* and *ethics*. Increasingly in what we might call the citizen of the future and indeed the present, there should be no distinction between being able to work with your hands and your mind. Entrepreneurialism is being able to resolve complex personal and societal challenges locally and globally. Entrepreneurialism does not just pertain to business endeavors. Every time a group tries to solve a social problem (youth crime, homelessness, bullying, and so on), they require the entrepreneurial skills of critical thinking, problem solving, innovative ideas, collaboration and communication, and the qualities of character.

The mark of an educated person is that of a *doer* (a doing-thinker; a thinker-doer)—they learn to do and do to learn. They are impatient with lack of action. Doing is not something they decide to do—daily life *is doing,* as natural as breathing the air. Along with doing is an exquisite awareness of the *ethics of life.* Small-scale ethics is how they treat others; large-scale ethics concern humankind and the evolution of the planet. When we change our education system and when hordes of people are acting individually and collectively in entrepreneurial and ethical ways, the world changes and keeps on changing with built-in adaptation. In these respects, a key characteristic about deep learning is that it is "in the moment." It embraces John Dewey's observation some 100 years ago that "education is not preparation for life, it is life." Thus, in the NPDL, the distinction between living and learning and schooling becomes blurred. Students are living and creating their own lives and futures through understanding and attempting to solve problems in their own communities and globally (Fullan & Scott, 2014).

This ability to meld and integrate the competencies was also reinforced in a recent blog, The Unexpected Path to Creative Breakthroughs, by Tim Brown, CEO of IDEO, an innovation and design firm. He reminds us to avoid the pressure to define ourselves as either humanities people or science people, either artists or geeks, or either intuitive or analytical types but to embrace both sides. He recounts examples from history—Leonardo da Vinci, Frank Gehry, and Steve Jobs—as people who reached across the divide of the arts and sciences as the starting point for bold innovation (Brown, 2015).

In the United States, the CCSS is another vehicle for building clarity of learning goals as they bring a common language and, if implemented effectively, a consistency of practice. One of our colleagues in the new pedagogies work has described the relationship between CCSS and NPDL in the following way: The CCSS outcomes dovetail well with those of the NPDL. One of the hallmark features of the CCSS is the opportunity for students to build knowledge about the world and other disciplines through text rather than their teacher. This process requires students to be able to read closely, think deeply, and learn independently. It shifts the role of the teacher from the keeper of knowledge to an activator of deep, meaningful learning. This represents a profound shift in instruction; rather than passively receiving knowledge and facts, students are expected to actively participate in their own education, independently applying their skills and knowledge. Essentially, teachers and students become partners in the learning process. The CCSS has the potential to provide clarity of learning goals (the "what"). The weakness of the CCSS is that in its current form, it does not provide the "how" for transforming the teaching and learning process. The NPDL and the CCSS are aligned in targeting the same learning competencies (the 6Cs), and they provide important insights on the "how." Using cutting-edge, innovative instructional strategies, teachers empower students to develop strong critical thinking skills such as interpretation, analysis, synthesis, and evaluation. Students will not only be able to think deeply and independently but also be able to articulate the "why" behind their learning. Students are stretched to use concepts rather than simply memorize them. Further, these strategies are based on the belief that if students are to flourish in the 21st century, they must take an active role in their own education (Hamilton, personal communication, November 2014).

It is clear that educators, businesses, and parents recognize that the traditional basics are not sufficient and that future generations need also the 6Cs if they are to thrive. What is critical for schools, districts, and education systems is not just defining the deep learning competencies but identifying their interrelationships, practices that foster progression in their development, and ways to cultivate and share those practices with consistency for all learners.

Build Precision in Pedagogy

Schools and districts that make sustained improvement in learning for all students develop explicit frameworks or models to guide the learning process. This *instructional guidance system* (Bryk, Bender Sebring, Allensworth, Luppescu, & Easton, 2010) is crucial because it represents the "black box" of implementation. The history of education is heavily weighted toward lofty goals and outcomes (usually poorly assessed) but weak on pedagogy. Our Coherence Framework makes pedagogical precision a priority and a driving force.

Instructional or pedagogical (we use the terms interchangeably) systems must include the development of at least the following four components:

- *Build a common language and knowledge base.* Cultivate system-wide engagement by involving all levels of the system to capture and create a model for learning and teaching. Identify the learning goals and principles that underlie the learning process. This collaborative approach builds language to promote meaningful conversations about practice.
- *Identify proven pedagogical practices.* The process typically begins with an analysis of best practices currently used in the district and

an examination of the research to validate the model. Ownership and commitment emerge at all levels of the system study, work, and learn together.

- *Build capacity.* Provide consistent and sustained capacity building based on research-proven practices to build precision in pedagogy. Teachers need "a deep multidimensional knowledge that allows them both to assess situations quickly and to draw upon a variety of repertoires for intervention. Individual teachers possess such knowledge but it is largely invisible to the field as a whole. There are few ways for it to be gathered, codified and shared" (Mehta, Schwartz, & Hess, 2012). Collective capacity building and the collaborative work processes in previous chapters make the knowledge and skills accessible and visible to all.

- *Provide clear causal links to impact.* Pedagogies should specify the two-way street between learning and assessment. Such a process serves to strengthen the specificity of instructional practice and its causal efficacy in making a difference to learning. This is what Hattie (2012) is getting at with his mantra "know thy impact." Knowing your impact is not just a matter of being responsible for outcomes but it also reverberates back to clarify how teaching and learning can be strengthened.

For the past decade, North America and the world have been focused on developing basic literacy and numeracy skills. These are foundational for learning, and they continue to be essential but are not sufficient to prepare our students for the complex world they will face. Schools, districts, and countries must find ways to sustain continuous improvement on the basics, while building innovative practices to develop what we call the deep learning competencies (defined previously). Implementing the promise of the CCSS for more critical thinking and problem solving and indeed joining the global digital world will require what we call the new pedagogies.

The concept of "simplexity" refers to the smallest number of potentially interrelated elements that feed on each other and achieve success. The secret to the NPDL lies in building teacher capacity to identify the interrelated pieces and, more importantly, to develop precision in how to combine them or make them gel to meet the varying needs of learners.

In the NPDL work, we have identified three strands of expertise that teachers need to weave together if they are to support deeper learning. These are precision in *pedagogical partnerships* that engage students in codesigning authentic relevant learning, *learning environments* that foster risk taking and 24/7 connections, and *leveraging digital* so it accelerates learning.

We examine each of the three strands of the NPDL depicted in Figure 4.3 and then consider an approach for building capacity to combine them.

Figure 4.3   The New Pedagogies

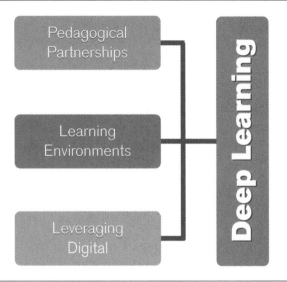

Pedagogical Partnerships

The first strand recognizes that teachers must possess deep expertise in instructional and assessment practices if they are to maximize the impact and use of digital to accelerate learning. These new pedagogies build on the foundation of proven pedagogical practices but fuse them with emerging innovative practices that foster the creation and application of new ideas and knowledge in real life. Educators must hone a deep knowledge of the learning process and a repertoire of strategies if they are to use digital as an accelerator. The magic is not in the device but in the scaffolding of experiences and challenges finely tuned to the needs and interests of students and maximized through relevance, authenticity, and real-world connections.

The first step in building precision in pedagogical practices begins with a culture that fosters learning for all. If the adults are not thinking at high levels, it is unlikely the students will be either. Districts and schools that get results have clarity about the elements of their instructional system. They build knowledge from the research combined with best practices in their context and then ensure that everyone has the skills and resources to apply them appropriately.

Schools and districts who want to build a common language and knowledge base and identify proven pedagogical practices may want to consider the work of John Hattie in *Visible Learning* (2009). He reviews the impact of instructional strategies and concludes that what is needed to raise the bar and close the gap is consensus and skill development by all teachers engaged with groups of students around the most impactful strategies. He differentiates the role of teachers as facilitators that has a .17 impact on learning with the role of teachers as activator at .87. The role of teachers as activators is far more powerful as it is more active in engaging student learning and challenging next practice.

We saw earlier that in his most recent research Hattie found that *collective efficacy* (now called *collaborative expertise*) of teachers had the highest impact of all of the 150 or so practices he examined. One can see as well in our definition of the new pedagogy as centered on the learning partnership between and among teachers, students, and families that collective efficacy for this trio of partners could be even more powerful.

In his findings around instructional strategies, a correlation of .40 or higher represents a year's growth in a year. Some notable high-impact strategies that would be in an activator's repertoire include the following:

Cognitive task analysis	.87
Giving feedback	.75
Teacher-student relationship	.72
Student expectations	1.44

Two underused strategies with tremendous power are giving feedback and student expectations. He reports that on average students get three to five seconds of precise feedback per day. What they need is feedback that helps them set the next challenge for their learning and the one after that.

Gaming is a good example of providing specific, timely feedback that challenges the student to consistently higher levels of performance. This requires teachers to move students from what they know toward explicit success criteria.

He also makes a distinction between strategies appropriate for shallow versus deep learning. *Shallow* learning he defines not as trivial or less important but learning that is essential to understand the content and develop basic skills. Shallow learning then becomes a foundation for *deeper* learning. Deeper learning is the ability to understand concepts, think critically, solve problems, and apply learning in authentic ways. Strategies for deeper learning include inquiry, problem-based learning, and knowledge production approaches. Not only are these strategies underutilized but they are often not used appropriately and fail to get the results they could.

These strategies and others clearly have the potential to close the gap if applied with fidelity and professional knowledge. What is crucial for schools and districts is an intentional strategy for cultivating collaborative cultures where teachers become more precise in knowing which strategy is most appropriate for that learner and that task.

No learning-teaching process is complete without addressing the black box of assessment. In our NPDL work we are not only identifying the pedagogies that affect learning but also creating new tools and measures for student success. We are shifting from measuring what is easy to measuring what matters. If we want students to develop the 6Cs of communication, critical thinking, collaboration, creativity, character, and citizenship, we need to be able to define and measure those competencies. To that end, we have created learning progressions that describe the pathway many students would follow in developing a competency. These tools become the anchor for meaningful discussion as groups of teachers design more meaningful learning based on the competencies; students and teachers develop success criteria, monitor progress, and evaluate growth. Teams of teachers then collaboratively examine student work and processes to analyze the quality of both the learning design and student progress. They use these data to identify the next appropriate learning challenge.

The pathway to change is accelerated when teachers engage in meaningful dialogue about effective practice using the strategies that provide the most impact. Collaborative examination of practice as described in

Chapter 3 increases this precision and causes teachers to raise their expectations for themselves and their students. This precision of pedagogical practice is essential as a foundation for deeper learning. We are seeing new relationships and ways of interacting beginning to emerge—what we call the new learning partnerships as teachers use their professional knowledge and expertise to engage and support learning with and among students in new ways.

The new pedagogies go deeper than changing pedagogy between students and teacher; they explore more deeply new roles for students. One of the most distinctive differences between traditional learning and the new pedagogies is the role students play and "the new learning partnerships" that emerge student to student, student to teacher, and student to the external world. New learning goals require changes in how relationships between students, teachers, families, and community are structured. The shift toward active learning partnerships requires students to take greater charge of their own and each other's learning inside and outside the classroom. The new learning partnerships have the potential to create more authentic and meaningful learning locally, nationally, and globally. This more active role increases student engagement. The shift to a new balance in decision making is inevitable because students are no longer willing to be passive recipients of learning defined by someone else, are digitally connected to massive amounts of new ideas and information, and respond to traditional didactic approaches with passivity once they have foundational skills.

Schools and districts that embrace the new learning partnership are seeing exponential growth in student engagement and success. We filmed recently in W. G. Davis Middle School in Ontario, where in 2009 students were disengaged, disruptive behaviors were on the rise, and achievement was dropping. The principal and staff collaborated over several months to find a solution. They eventually determined that their students needed better role models and the kind of digital engagement they valued outside the school. They realized that they were the ones who had to become role models for their students. This began a process of implementing more authentic learning using problem-based units that crossed traditional content boundaries and implementing a new bring your own device (BYOD) policy. The shift to cross-disciplinary planning and increased technology use caused teachers to move outside their comfort zone. They began using new strategies for coplanning and using digital resources supporting one another and feeling supported to take risks and even fail at first. Almost immediately, they noticed their roles with students were changing dramatically. Students were more engaged and teacher time in the classroom was spent on giving feedback and challenging the next step in learning rather than in delivering content. As they focused on meaningful, relevant learning using what we are calling the new pedagogies, they also saw more than a 20 percent leap in reading and writing scores over three years on the provincial testing (Video: W. G. Davis, www.michaelfullan.ca).

The new learning partnerships we saw at W. G. Davis take time and expertise to develop. Meaningful learning partnerships with students can be accelerated when teachers understand the three elements of the student learning model, depicted in Figure 4.4.

This model goes beyond the notions of student voice and agency to combine both internal development and external connections to the world. We are not talking here about student forums or interest surveys (although they may be part of the approach) but about a deeper engagement of students

Figure 4.4   Student Learning Model

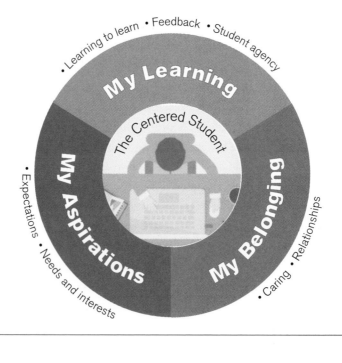

as codesigners and colearners. The three elements of the model all contribute to the development of students as active, engaged learners who are prepared to learn for life and experience learning as life. Educators need to be aware of these key elements to design learning and environments that maximize student potential to thrive. Moreover—and this is crucial—none of these three components are fixed variables. They can be altered through intervention. This domain represents a vastly underutilized set of factors that would be very high yield (low cost, high impact). The student learning model then focuses on the three elements of student development and ways they become active participants in my learning, my belonging, and my aspirations.

My Learning

The first element refers to the need for students to take responsibility for their learning and to understand the process of learning, if it is to be maximized. This requires students to develop skills in *learning to learn,* giving and receiving *feedback,* and enacting *student agency.*

- Learning to learn requires that students build metacognition about their learning. They begin to define their own learning goals and success criteria; monitor their own learning and critically examine their work; and incorporate feedback from peers, teachers, and others to deepen their awareness of how they function in the learning process.
- Feedback is essential to improving performance. As students make progress in mastering the learning process, the role of the teacher gradually shifts from explicitly structuring the learning task, toward providing feedback, activating the next learning challenge, and continuously developing the learning environment.
- Student agency emerges as students take a more active role in codeveloping learning tasks and assessing results. It is more than participation; it is engaging students in real decision making and a willingness to learn together.

My Belonging

The second element of belonging is a crucial foundation for all human beings who are social by nature and crave purpose, meaning, and connectedness to others.

- *Caring* environments help students to flourish and meet the basic need of all humans to feel they are respected and belong.
- *Relationships* are integral to preparing for authentic learning. As students develop both interpersonal connections and intrapersonal insight, they are able to move to successively more complex tasks in groups and independently. Managing collaborative relationships and being self-monitoring are skills for life.

My Aspirations

Student results can be dramatically affected by the expectations they hold of themselves and the perceptions they believe others have for them (see also Quaglia & Corso, 2014).

- *Expectations* are a key determinant of success, as noted in Hattie's research. Students must believe they can achieve and also feel that others believe that. They must codetermine success criteria and be engaged in measuring their growth. Families, students, and teachers can together foster higher expectations through deliberate means— sometimes simply by discussing current and ideal expectations and what might make them possible to achieve.
- *Needs and interests* are a powerful accelerator for motivation and engagement. Teachers who tap into the natural curiosity and interest of students are able to use that as a springboard to deeply engage students in tasks that are relevant, authentic, and examine concepts and problems in depth.

Teachers, schools, and districts that combine strategies to unlock the three elements in their students will foster untapped potential and form meaningful learning partnerships.

Learning Environments

The second strand that fosters the transformation to deep learning is a shift in the learning environment. Quality learning environments that use the pedagogical practices and build the learning partnerships described previously need to meet four criteria: be irresistibly engaging for students and teachers, allow 24/7 access to learning, cultivate social learning, and foster risk taking and innovation. Students thrive in this type of learning environment and so do teachers.

How, then, do we transform today's classrooms from the traditional status quo to places of energy, curiosity, imagination, and deep learning? A recent video by the inventor of the Rubik's cube, Erno Rubik, sheds light on the dilemma when he asks, "How do we get teachers to stop teaching answers but instead to help students generate questions that are waiting for answers?"

There is no one recipe for creating classrooms that provoke deep learning, but as we look across the early innovators we see a few common characteristics. In schools on the pathway to deepening learning, we see the following:

- *Students asking the questions.* They have skills and language to pursue inquiry and are not passively taking in the answers from teachers.
- *Questions valued above answers.* The process of learning, discovering, and conveying is as important as the end result.
- *Varied models for learning.* Selection of approaches is matched to student needs and interests. Students are supported to reach for the next challenge.
- *Explicit connections to real-world application.* Learning designs are not left to chance but scaffolded and built on relevance and meaning.
- *Collaboration.* Students possess skills to collaborate within the classroom and beyond.
- *Assessment of learning that is embedded, transparent, and authentic.* Students define personal goals, monitor progress toward success criteria, and engage in feedback with peers and others.

Attention to these criteria will create learning environments where students can flourish. Schools, districts, and systems should consider the degree to which they are providing conditions that support this type of learning environment.

Leveraging Digital

The third strand of the deep learning trio is leveraging digital. We have purposely moved away from the term *technology* to signal that this discussion is not about devices but about learning that can be amplified, accelerated, and facilitated by interaction with the digital world. This demands a rethinking of the ways we use technology. It's not about putting a device in front of every student and leaving them to learn independently. That will only result in students who are digital isolates. It is about bringing the digital world inside the process of learning and building collaboration, within and outside the classroom, in ways that are authentic and relevant.

Alan November (2012), a pioneer in the meaningful use of technology for over three decades, describes this new view of the digital world as "transforming learning beyond the $1000 pencil." Just adding devices is not enough; mind-sets and behaviors need to change for both students and teachers. He emphasizes that students must be taught how to use technology appropriately, safely, and ethically to gain understanding at the highest levels (Bloom's taxonomy or depth of knowledge). Teachers then "guide students in the complex tasks of innovation and problem solving, and in doing work that makes a contribution to the learning processes of others" (November, 2012, p. 18).

In his book *Who Owns the Learning?* November challenges educators to ask themselves six questions to determine if they are getting beyond the superficial use of digital:

1. Did the assignment build capacity for critical thinking on the web?

2. Did the assignment develop new lines of inquiry?

3. Are there opportunities to broaden the perspective of the conversation with authentic audiences from around the world?

4. Is there an opportunity for students to publish—across various media with capacity for continuous feedback?

5. Is there an opportunity for students to create a contribution (purposeful work)?

6. Does the assignment demo "best in the world" examples of content and skill?

The challenge for leaders is to help educators move from uses of technology as substitution to uses of digital that provide value. If I'm a student studying a unit on poverty and I use technology to create a PowerPoint instead of handwriting a report, there may be little value added. In contrast, if I interview people in four global communities who are living in poverty, synthesize that information, and create my report, there has been tremendous value added through the layers of critical thinking, communication, character, and global citizenship.

Making the New Pedagogies "Gel"

Building capacity in all three strands of the new pedagogies takes persistence and commitment. We find a good example of sustained focus that gets new and better results in our work with Napa Valley Unified School District. The district is making progress in building on powerful pedagogical practices—particularly problem-based learning and leveraging digital. Napa has developed a clear instructional focus on what they term their 4Cs and combines that with growing use of digital. The approach began more than a decade ago at New Tech High but has evolved to engage the entire district. Napa intentionally built the capacity of teachers in every school, over time, to use the new pedagogy and then used the addition of digital devices to enrich the thinking and learning. They have taken an approach to innovation by starting with some schools but using that learning in rapid cycles of reflection and doing to diffuse the learning to all schools. Each year they host an "Educators Exchange" to share the knowledge they are gaining with their schools but also laterally with other school districts.

Schools and districts need to foster collaborative inquiry into the three strands of the new pedagogies: pedagogical partnerships, learning environments, and leveraging digital. There is no simple recipe; this is a job for professional educators who must develop the expertise and knowledge base that is a foundation for fostering deeper learning. The simplexity is knowing the elements and integrating them so that every child has the learning experience that challenges and supports them. The challenge for schools and districts is to build momentum across all classrooms.

Shift Practices Through Capacity Building

Once districts and schools have clarified the learning goals and developed precision in pedagogical practices, they must focus on the "how" of shifting practice. They need to identify the processes that will support a shift in practice for *all* educators. We will highlight the key attributes and then illustrate with examples in action.

As we look at districts that are making the shift to support deep learning, we see that several conditions are in place. Superintendents and principals shift behaviors on a large scale when they combine the strategies noted in Chapter 3.

- They model being lead learners. They don't send people to capacity building sessions but learn alongside them.
- They shape a culture that fosters an expectation of learning for everyone, taking risks and making mistakes but learning from them.
- They build capacity vertically and horizontally in the organization with persistence and single-mindedness until it affects learning.

How do schools and districts tackle the shift to deep learning?

The first step in making a change is to assess the starting point. We offer a few questions for reflection about your capacity to shift the practices in your school, district, or state.

Assessing Capacity

Teachers:

1. Do teachers possess knowledge and skills in pedagogical practices?

2. Do teachers have knowledge and skills to develop new learning partnerships?

3. Do teachers have the knowledge and skills to create learning environments that move beyond the traditional classroom?

4. Do teachers have the knowledge and skills to use digital resources to accelerate learning?

Schools:

1. Do school leaders have the knowledge and skills to create a culture of learning for teachers and students?

2. Do schools have collaborative learning structures and process?

3. Do schools have access to models of effective practice and opportunities to share laterally and vertically?

Districts:

1. Does the district have clarity of learning goals?

2. Have high-yield pedagogical practices been identified and shared?

3. Does the district create a culture of learning for all educators?

4. Does the district provide resources for collaborative learning structures and processes to thrive?

We use examples to illustrate how schools and districts can use the elements of the Coherence Framework to assess their starting point and then either focus on continuous improvement of the basic literacies or sustain those basics while innovating with deeper learning.

The first school example is Cochrane Collegiate Academy in North Carolina that in 2008 lacked clarity of goals, had little precision or consistency in pedagogy, and had weak capacity and culture to support change. They needed to focus relentlessly on continuous improvement of the basics. The second school example is Park Manor Senior Public School in Ontario, which had some clarity of goals, good pedagogy, and teacher capacity but was underperforming. They combined continuous improvement with innovating with deep learning and digital and saw their writing scores soar.

Cochrane Collegiate Academy

We look first to a school that was able to engage an underperforming student population with dramatic results using pedagogical precision and capacity building. In 2007, Cochrane Collegiate Academy in Charlotte, North Carolina, was listed as one of the 30 lowest-performing schools in North Carolina. By 2011, the number of students performing at grade level had doubled and the achievement gap had been reduced by 35 percent in reading and math. Most notable was that their growth was 3.5 times that of North Carolina in mathematics and twice the rate of growth in reading.

Cochrane serves a population of 640 students in grades 6 through 8. Eighty-seven percent qualify for free or reduced lunch, 60 percent are

African American, and 30 percent are Latino. In a recent Edutopia (n.d.) video, teachers described the situation in 2008 as out of control with students running and screaming in the halls, weak performance at 20 percent in reading and math, and good teachers choosing to leave the profession.

Staff attribute their success to their principal who brought out their potential using five key components:

1. Use quality professional development that is research based, consistent, convenient, relevant, and differentiated.

2. Use time wisely by flipping faculty meeting time to focus on learning, not administration.

3. Trust your teachers to determine the professional learning they need next.

4. Facilitate, don't dictate by providing teachers with what they need and allowing them to make decisions.

5. Expect the best by holding everyone to high standards.

Guided by research, they identified their top 10 teaching practices and engaged weekly in professional learning to help them implement the practices more effectively. Their nonnegotiable list of strategies included the following: essential questions, activating strategy, relevant vocabulary, limited lecture, graphic organizer, student movement, higher-order thinking questions, summarize, rigorous, and student centered.

What differentiates this school is not which top 10 instructional strategies they selected but the fact that they built a common language, knowledge base, and set of practices about quality learning and teaching. They instituted practices and processes such as weekly professional learning targeted to this instructional guidance system. Strong professional relationships, collaborative work, and learning partnerships with their students are making the difference. They have work still to be done but are on a trajectory for success.

Park Manor Senior Public School

The second school example is Park Manor, which serves grades 6, 7, and 8 students just outside of Toronto. It is a normal school with the same standard resources of all schools in that district. In *Stratosphere* (2013c), Fullan profiled the innovations at Park Manor for two reasons. First, they increased scores on the Ontario assessment, which measures higher-order skills, from 42 percent to 83 percent in just four years. Second, they applied what we are calling the three strands of the new pedagogies to shift practice across the entire school.

Park Manor's stated mission is to develop "global critical thinkers collaborating to change the world." The goal is clear and concise, and it is shared by everyone. Many schools have inspiring goals, but Park Manor was an early innovator in developing a clear strategy for moving forward. Their approach was to build a collaborative culture that was learning together how to do this work. James Bond, the principal, and Liz Anderson, the learning coordinator, facilitated a process where they and the teachers developed clarity about what learning needed to be like to serve their students. They developed as a staff what they call an *accelerated learning framework* to guide the transition from goals to action (see Figure 4.5).

Over a two-year period, they developed several versions of the framework and still see it as a work in progress. Teachers explained the following:

> We begin with the student and then embed the 6Cs into everything. From there we develop the learning goals, success criteria, rich learning tasks and then make decisions about the pedagogy that is most appropriate. Only then, do we consider the digital tools and resources that will accelerate the learning. (Video at www.michaelfullan.ca)

While they are committed to incorporating digital, they learned early on that pedagogy had to be the driver with digital acting as an accelerator. Visitors to the school are always impressed that every student can articulate their learning goals and success criteria, the reasons for the digital or pedagogical strategy they may be using, and how the tools are meeting their learning needs.

Three indicators of success have evolved: first, gains in student achievement have been significant; second, the school uses success criteria and evidence to determine the effectiveness of the framework as

Figure 4.5 The Accelerated Learning Model—Park Manor PS

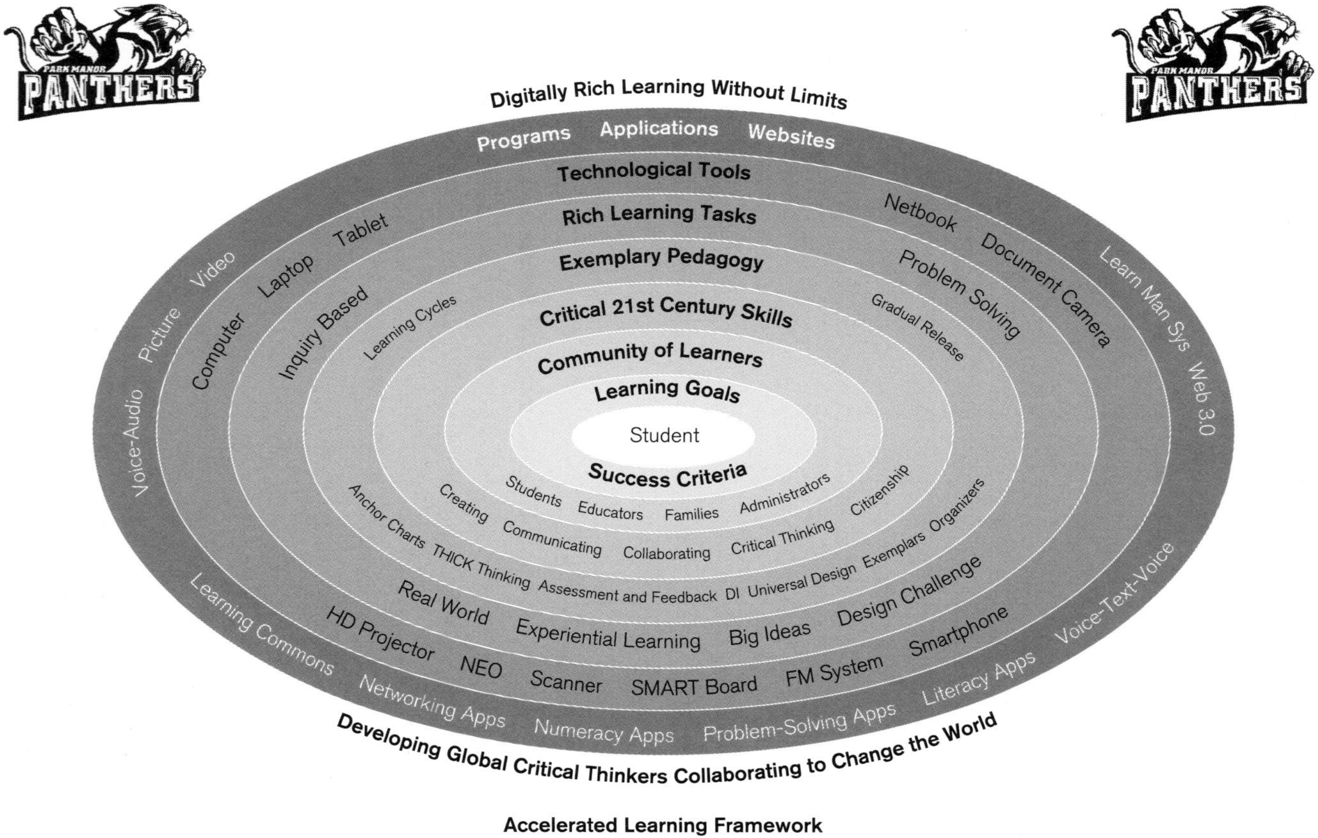

Source: Created by Liz Anderson and James Bond. Courtesy of Park Manor Senior Public School.

it relates to student learning; and third, the notion of developing a learning framework has been taken up by other schools across North America. Schools and districts are seeing the development of a learning framework as a powerful process to build shared language, knowledge, and expertise. The framework serves to clarify the small number of goals, identify the pedagogical practices that need to be in every teacher's repertoire, and provide a focus for capacity building that gets results.

Moving Whole Systems Toward Deeper Learning

In Chapter 2, we described a large-scale transformation in Ontario, Canada, where they significantly improved learning in an entire province—5,000 public schools—by using the elements of the Coherence Framework: focusing direction, cultivating collaborative cultures, deepening learning, and securing accountability. They have developed considerable consistency of pedagogical practices across the 5,000 schools. They are sustaining the continuous improvement but simultaneously focusing on more innovative practices to leverage digital. At the district level, we have referenced examples such as York Region, Long Beach, and Garden Grove that have intentionally focused on consistency of practice and are now moving toward the innovation side. This resulted from attending to the pedagogical precision combined with a collaborative culture that fosters risk taking and an infrastructure that will support the new approaches both in policy and practice.

One of the few examples of "whole system" improvement using digital is Mooresville, North Carolina (Edwards, 2015). Based on principles aligned with our work, Superintendent Mark Edwards has used leadership, pedagogy, and collaborative cultures to transform the culture and performance of a district of 6,000 students and 9 schools. To take but one indicator—the state's Annual Measurable Objectives—Mooresville has gone from being one of the lowest-performing districts to becoming the highest-performing in the state, despite having one of the lowest per pupil budgets. In short, success is possible by employing the small number of key principles and implementing them well and persistently, learning and adapting as you go.

We began the chapter by suggesting the time is ripe for a revolution in learning. Robust examples of whole districts that are successful on the innovation side of deep learning are not yet visible. We are following districts and countries that are exploring the intersection of pedagogy and digital. One global partnership, NPDL, is particularly promising. Hundreds of schools in countries including Australia/New Zealand, Canada, Finland, the Netherlands, Uruguay, and the United States are blending a focus on strong pedagogy with innovation to accelerate student learning leveraged by digital. Equally important, they are using the whole system approach to change by providing enabling conditions at the school, district, and country levels for innovation to flourish. This is an innovation laboratory for building and sharing knowledge about what deep learning is, how we get more of it, and how we measure these crucial competencies. We look forward to reporting on this growing social movement to transform learning.

Final Thoughts

Coherence is on everyone's radar. Leaders at the school, district, and state levels recognize that the piecemeal efforts of the past will not allow them to meet the promise of CCSS or the needs of their students. You will recall our reference in Chapter 1 to the study by Susan Moore Johnson and her colleagues (2015) of how five districts achieved greater coherence and concluded that success was not a matter of the degree of centralization or decentralization but rather the quality of implementation. In both scenarios, effectiveness required strong vertical and horizontal trust and partnerships.

As we look at those five districts and other schools, states, and districts cited in this book, it becomes clear that the pathway to success for students is not about size of districts or schools, centralization versus decentralization, poverty versus privilege, or one program versus another. The pattern that emerges is consistent with our framework for coherence.

First, all of these examples had a clear and shared focused direction. They articulated a small number of goals directly linked to improved student learning and then persisted in working toward them. Often, the stimulus was an urgency to respond to serious issues of poverty and/or underachievement. In every case, this was not a simple solution but a concerted effort of committed leadership at all levels, over multiple years—it's hard work and not for the faint of heart.

Second, they built a collaborative culture by focusing on capacity building. They fostered strong relationships with teachers, leaders, and community. They recognize that lateral capacity (connecting and learning across schools) and vertical connection (good relationships between central office and principals and teachers) to the overall agenda forms the glue of coherence.

Third, they have a deep commitment to the learning and teaching nexus. They are not looking for a quick fix but rather to create collaborative communities of inquiry that deeply examine instructional practices and student results. Some are focused on getting the foundational literacies in place while others are tackling the deeper learning agenda accelerated by the digital world. In these places of deep learning for the adults as well as the students, there is a professionalism that permeates relationships and decisions so that they propel the learning agenda.

The elements of the Coherence Framework do not operate in isolation; rather, success depends on the synergy of their integration—seeking the combination that makes the elements gel, knowing that coherence will never be achieved as an end state but will always need to be sought. You can become better at it, achieve greater degrees of coherence, and you will end up—with a greater coherence making capacity in your system. Focusing direction gets us into the game, cultivating collaborative cultures provides the pathway for change, and deepening learning is the core strategy for affecting student results. We turn next to the fourth element, securing accountability, which is essential if we are to measure and achieve growth in meaningful ways and be accountable to ourselves and the public.

Review the contents of this chapter using Infographic 4 before proceeding to Chapter 5, Securing Accountability.

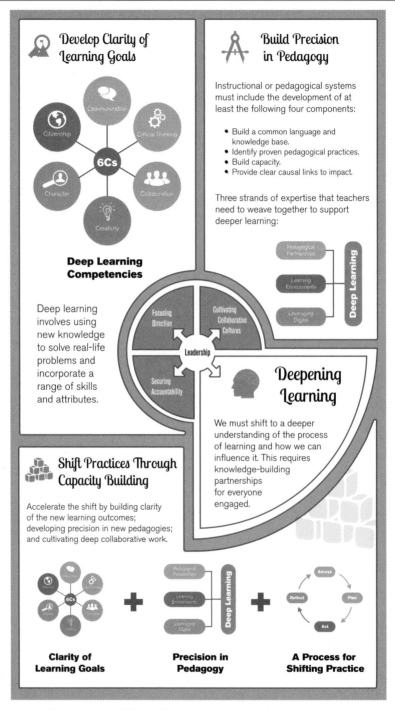

Develop Clarity of Learning Goals

Deep Learning Competencies

6Cs
- Communication
- Citizenship
- Critical Thinking
- Character
- Collaboration
- Creativity

Deep learning involves using new knowledge to solve real-life problems and incorporate a range of skills and attributes.

Build Precision in Pedagogy

Instructional or pedagogical systems must include the development of at least the following four components:

- Build a common language and knowledge base.
- Identify proven pedagogical practices.
- Build capacity.
- Provide clear causal links to impact.

Three strands of expertise that teachers need to weave together to support deeper learning:

Deep Learning
- Pedagogical Partnerships
- Learning Environments
- Leveraging Digital

Leadership
- Focusing Direction
- Cultivating Collaborative Cultures
- Securing Accountability

Deepening Learning

We must shift to a deeper understanding of the process of learning and how we can influence it. This requires knowledge-building partnerships for everyone engaged.

Shift Practices Through Capacity Building

Accelerate the shift by building clarity of the new learning outcomes; developing precision in new pedagogies; and cultivating deep collaborative work.

Clarity of Learning Goals

6Cs

+

Precision in Pedagogy

Deep Learning
- Pedagogical Partnerships
- Learning Environments
- Leveraging Digital

+

A Process for Shifting Practice

- Assess
- Plan
- Act
- Reflect

 A full-color version of this infographic is also available for download at **http://www.corwin.com/ books/Book244044** under "About" and then "Sample Materials and Chapters."

5

Securing Accountability

Earlier we called accountability the big bugbear, and it is. And when you think of it, sorting out accountability is as basic as humankind (think of raising your children, relationships between spouses, your own personal sense of responsibility). People in charge have tried to solve the accountability problem directly (put out the garbage or you will be grounded Saturday night). As we saw from Daniel Pink, the "carrots and sticks" approach does not work for anything that requires initiative, judgment, and ongoing commitment.

We have been working for years on how to position accountability to be an effective component of school and system change. Recently, we brought these ideas together in an article on collective accountability (Fullan, Rincón-Gallardo, & Hargreaves, 2015) and for individual accountability (Fullan, 2015). We draw heavily on these accounts in this chapter.

The argument is this: If you want effective accountability, you need to develop conditions that maximize *internal accountability*—conditions that increase the likelihood that people will be accountable to themselves and to the group. Second, you need to frame and reinforce internal accountability with *external accountability*—standards, expectations, transparent data, and selective interventions. This chapter describes how this internal-external dynamic works and the evidence that this is the best approach for the fourth component of the Coherence Framework: securing accountability (see Figure 5.1).

Figure 5.1 Securing Accountability

•••

Internal Accountability

Simply stated, accountability is taking responsibility for one's actions. At the core of accountability in educational systems is student learning. As City, Elmore, Fiarman, and Teitel (2009) argue, "the real accountability system is in the tasks that students are asked to do" (p. 23). Constantly improving and refining instructional practice so that students can engage in deep learning tasks is perhaps the single most important responsibility of the teaching profession and educational systems as a whole. In this sense, accountability as defined here is not limited to mere gains in test scores but on deeper and more meaningful learning for all students.

Internal accountability occurs when individuals and groups willingly take on personal, professional, and collective responsibility for continuous improvement and success for all students (Hargreaves & Shirley, 2009).

External accountability is when system leaders reassure the public through transparency, monitoring, and selective intervention that their system is performing in line with societal expectations and requirements. The priority for policy makers, we argue, should be to lead with creating the conditions for internal accountability, because they are more effective in achieving greater overall accountability, including external accountability. Policy makers also have direct responsibilities to address external accountability, but this latter function will be far more effective if they get the internal part right.

Existing research on school and system effectiveness and improvement (DuFour & Eaker, 1998; Marzano, 2003; Pil & Leana, 2006; Zavadsky, 2009) and our own work with educational systems in the United States and internationally (Fullan, 2010; Hargreaves & Fullan, 2012; Hargreaves & Shirley, 2009) suggests that internal accountability must *precede* external accountability if lasting improvement in student achievement is the goal.

Richard Elmore (2004) conducted a series of intensive case studies of individual schools—some that failed to improve and some that improved their performance. Relative to the former, schools that failed to improve were not able to achieve instructional coherence, despite being in systems with strong external accountability. A minority of schools did develop internal coherence together and showed progress on student achievement. The main feature of successful schools was that they built a collaborative culture that combined individual responsibility, collective expectations, and corrective action—that is, internal accountability. Transparent data on instructional practices and student achievement were a feature of these cultures. As these cultures developed, they were also able to more effectively engage the external assessment system. Highlighting the fundamental role of internal accountability on school improvement, Elmore (2004) pointed out the following:

> It seems unlikely to us that schools operating in the default mode—where all questions of accountability related to student learning are essentially questions of individual teacher responsibility—will be capable of responding to strong obtrusive accountability systems in ways that lead to systematic deliberate

improvement of instruction and student learning. The idea that a school will *improve*, and therefore, the overall performance of its students, implies a capacity for collective deliberation and action that schools in our sample did not exhibit. Where virtually all decisions about accountability are made by individual teachers, based on their individual conceptions of what they and their students can do, it seems unlikely that these decisions will somehow aggregate into overall improvement for the school. (p. 197)

Internal accountability is based on the notion that individuals *and* the group in which they work can transparently hold themselves responsible for their performance. We already know that current external accountability schemes do not work because, at best, they tell us that the system is not performing but do not give a clue about *how* to fix the situation. As Elmore (2004) observes, if people do not know how to fix the problem and so cannot do so, then the following will occur:

Schools will implement the requirements of the external accountability system in pro forma ways without ever internalizing the values of responsibility and efficacy that are the nominal objectives of those systems. (p. 134)

Elmore (2004) then concludes this:

Investments in internal accountability *must logically precede* [emphasis added] any expectation that schools will respond productively to external pressure for performance. (p. 134)

"Logically precede," yes, but more to the point of our framework, internal accountability must *strategically* precede engagement with external accountability. This is why focusing direction, cultivating collaborative cultures, and deepening learning precede accountability in our Coherence Framework.

There are two messages here: One is that policy makers and other leaders are well advised to establish conditions for developing cultures of internal accountability. The second is that there are things other people can do when the hierarchy is not inclined to move. The answer is to "help make it happen in your own situation"—that is, develop collaborative work with your peers and push upward for this work to be supported.

The history of the teaching profession is laced with assumptions of and conditions for isolated, individual responsibility. But atomistic responsibility, detached from any group, can never work. In a nutshell, the cultural shift needed is to shift to collaborative cultures that honor and align individual responsibility with collective expectations and actions.

Elmore discusses several schools that he and his team studied. Most of them exemplify the individualistic model. Teachers work away on their own and periodically grapple or clash with external accountability requirements. But Elmore also discusses two cases where the schools have developed more or less "collaborative" cultures. The first case is St. Aloysius Elementary School:

> Without exception, teachers described an atmosphere of high expectations. Some stressed a high priority on "reaching every child" and "making sure that no one is left behind" while others referred to a serious and supportive environment where everyone is expected to put forth excellent work. (Elmore, 2004, p. 164)

It sounds ideal, but what happens when things don't go as expected? At another school, Turtle Haven, Elmore (2004) asked teachers, "What happens when teachers do not meet the collective expectations?" He reports that "most teachers believed that a person who did not meet . . . expectations, or conform to a culture created by those expectations would first receive a great deal of support from the principal and other colleagues" (p. 183).

If this approach failed to produce results, most Turtle Haven teachers said that the teacher in question would not be happy at the school and eventually would either "weed themselves out [or] eventually . . . if there was a sense in the community that a certain number of children were not able to get the kind of education that we say we're committed to providing . . . we would have to think whether the somebody belongs here or not" (Elmore, 2004, p. 183).

This kind of culture is not foolproof, but we would say it stacks up well against the external accountability thinking that creates demands that go unheeded or can't be acted on. In the collaborative cultures, the internal accountability system is based on visible expectations combined with consequences for failure to meet set expectations.

Such cultures, says Elmore (2004), are much better equipped to deal with external accountability requirements, adding that a school with a strong internal accountability culture might respond to external assessments in a number of ways, "including accepting and internalizing it; rejecting it and developing defenses against it, or incorporating just those elements of the system that the school or the individuals deem relevant" (p. 145).

What is coming through in this discussion is that collaborative cultures with an eye to continuous improvement establish internal processes that allow them to sort out differences and to make effective decisions. At the level of the microdynamics of school improvement, Elmore (2004) draws the same conclusion we do at the system level: investing in the conditions that develop internal accountability is more important than beefing up external accountability.

The Ontario Reform Strategy, which we discussed in previous chapters, offers an illustrative example of the importance of internal accountability preceding external accountability systemwide. The Canadian province of Ontario, with 4,900 schools in 72 districts serving some two million students, started in 2004 to invest in building capacity and internal accountability at the school and district levels. The initial impulse for the reform came from leadership at the top of the education system—Dalton McGuinty, the premier of the province at the time—through the establishment of a small number of ambitious goals related to improvements in literacy, numeracy, and high school retention. However, the major investments focused on strengthening the collective capacity of teachers, school principals, and district leaders to create the conditions for improved instructional practice and student achievement (Glaze, Mattingley, & Andrews, 2013).

There was little overt external accountability in the early stages of the Ontario Reform Strategy. External accountability measures were gradually introduced in the form of assessment results in grades 3 and 6 in literacy and numeracy, and in high school, retention numbers, transparency of data, and a school turnaround support-focused policy called Ontario Focused Intervention Program (OFIP) for schools that were underperforming. This system has yielded positive and measurable results in literacy that has improved dramatically across the 4,000 elementary schools and in high school graduation rates that have climbed from 68 percent to 84 percent across the 900 high schools. The number of OFIP schools, originally at over 800, has been reduced to 69 schools even after the criteria to identify a school as in need of intervention had widened to include many more schools (Glaze et al., 2013; Mourshed, Chijioke, & Barber, 2010).

An evaluation of the reform strategy in 10 of Ontario's 72 school districts that concentrated particularly on the special education aspects of the reform pointed to significant narrowing of the achievement gap in writing scores for students with learning disabilities (Hargreaves & Braun, 2012). Concerns were expressed among teachers who were surveyed about some of the deleterious consequences of standardized testing in grades 3 and 6— that the tests came at the end of the year at a point that was too late to serve a diagnostic function, that they were not sufficiently differentiated in order to match differentiated instructional strategies, and that principals in some schools placed undue emphasis on "bubble kids" near the baseline for proficiency rather than on students who struggled the most with literacy. Perhaps predictably, administrators who were surveyed at the school and system levels were more supportive of the standardized assessments.

The most intriguing finding though was that special education resource teachers, whose role was moving increasingly to providing in-class support, welcomed the presence of transparent objective data. They saw it as a way of drawing the attention of regular classroom teachers to the fact and the finding that students with learning disabilities could, with the right support, register valid and viable gains in measurable student achievement. Together, these findings point to the need to review the nature and form of high-stakes assessments—more differentiated, more just-in-time, and more directed at the needs of all students, perhaps—but also to the value of having transparent data that concentrate everyone's attention on supporting all students' success along with diagnostic data and collaborative professional responsibility for all students' learning, development, and success.

A similar approach to whole system improvement can be found in U.S. districts that have been awarded the prestigious Broad Prize for Urban Education, granted to urban school districts that demonstrate the greatest overall performance and improvement while reducing achievement gaps based on race, ethnicity, and income. In her in-depth study of five such districts, Zavadsky (2009) finds that, while diverse in context and strategies, these districts have addressed the challenge of improving student performance systemwide following remarkably similar approaches: investing in, growing, and circulating the professional capital of schools (what they term *building capacity*) to improve instructional practice by fostering teacher collaboration and collective accountability. These successful schools set high instructional targets, attracting and developing talent, aligning resources to key improvement priorities, constantly monitoring progress, and providing timely targeted supports when needed.

The solid and mounting evidence on the fundamental impact of internal accountability on the effectiveness and improvement of schools and school systems contrasts sharply with the scarce or null evidence that external accountability, by itself or as the prime driver, can bring about lasting and sustained improvements in student and school performance. There is, indeed, a growing realization that external accountability is not an effective driver of school and system effectiveness. At best, external accountability does not get its intended results. At worst, it produces undesirable and sometimes unconscionable consequences, such as the cheating scandal in Atlanta (Hill, 2015).

We frequently ask successful practitioners that we work with how they themselves handle the "accountability dilemma" (direct accountability doesn't work; indirect may be too soft). What follows are a few responses that we have personally received to this question: What is effective accountability? Not surprisingly, these views are entirely consistent with Elmore (2004):

> Accountability is now primarily described as an accountability for student learning. It is less about some test result and more about accepting ownership of the moral imperative of having every student learn. Teachers talk about "monitoring" differently. As they engage in greater sharing of the work, they talk about being accountable as people in the school community know what they are doing and looking to see what is changing for students as a result. And as they continue to deprivatize teaching, they talk about their principal and peers coming into their classrooms and expecting to see the work [of agreed-upon practices] reflected in their teaching, their classroom walls, and student work. (Anonymous, personal communication, November 2014)

Teachers and administrators talk about accountability by deprivatizing their practice. If everyone knows what the other teacher or administrator is working on and how they are working on it with students, it becomes a lot easier to talk about accountability. When everyone has an understanding of accountability, creating clear goals and steps to reach those goals, it makes it easier for everyone to talk and work in accountable environments. (Elementary principal, personal communication, November 2014)

I spoke with my staff about accountability versus responsibility in brainstorming, about what is our purpose and who is responsible for what . . . being explicit and letting teachers collectively determine what our responsibilities are. (Secondary school principal, personal communication, November 2014)

We are moving to define accountability as responsibility. My district has been engaged in some important work that speaks to intrinsic motivation, efficacy, perseverance, etc., and accountability is seen as doing what is best for students . . . working together to tackle any challenge and being motivated by our commitment as opposed to some external direction. (Superintendent, personal communication, November 2014)

When you blow down the doors and walls, you can't help but be evermore accountable. (Superintendent, personal communication, November 2014)

I do believe that a lot of work remains to be done on building common understanding on the notion of accountability. Many people still believe that someone above them in the hierarchy is accountable. Very few take personal accountability for student learning and achievement. There are still those who blame parents and students' background for achievement. (Consultant, personal communication, November 2014)

In one school, the talk about accountability was pervasive as the school became designated as underperforming. The morale of the school went down significantly, and the tension was omnipresent at every meeting. The team switched the conversation to motivation, innovation, and teamwork and the culture changed. The school is energized and the test scores went up in one year. The team is now committed to results and continuous improvement. (Consultant, personal communication, November 2014)

In short, internal accountability is far more effective than external accountability. The bottom line is that it produces forceful accountability in a way that no hierarchy can possibly match. We have shown this to be the case for teachers, and we can make the parallel argument for students. If we want students to be more accountable, we need to change instruction toward methods that increase individual students' responsibility for assessing their own learning and for students to work in peer groups to assess and provide feedback to each other under the guidance of the teacher. We still need external accountability, and we can now position it more effectively.

External Accountability

External accountability concerns any entity that has authority over you. Its presence is still essential, but we need to reposition external accountability so that it becomes more influential in the performance of individuals, groups, and the system as a whole. We first take the perspective of external authorities and then flip back to local entities.

External Authorities

The first thing to note is that if the external body invests in building widespread internal accountability they will be furthering their own goals of greater organization or system accountability. The more that internal accountability thrives, the greater the responsiveness to external requirements and the less the externals have to do. When this happens, the center has less need to resort to carrots and sticks to incite the system to act responsibly.

Dislodging top-down accountability from its increasingly miscast role has turned out to be exceedingly difficult. People at the top do not like to give up control. They cling to it despite obvious evidence that it does not work. And attacks on the inadequacy of top-down account-ability have failed because they have only focused on the "from" side of freedom. Critics seem to be saying that accountability requirements do not work, so remove them. That is not the complete solution because it takes us back to nothing. The answer is found in our argument in this chapter—rely on developing the conditions for internal accountability and reinforce them with certain aspects of external accountability. In particular, central authorities should focus their efforts on two inter-related activities:

1. Investing in internal accountability

2. Projecting and protecting the system

By the first I mean investing in the conditions that cause internal accountability to get stronger. The beauty of this approach, as we have seen, is that people throughout the system start doing the work of accountability. Though indirect, this form of accountability is really more explicit, more present, and, of course, more effective. We have already suggested its components:

- A small number of ambitious goals, processes that foster shared goals (and even targets if jointly shaped)
- Good data that are used primarily for developmental purposes
- Implementation strategies that are transparent, whereby people and organizations are grouped to learn from each other (using the group to change the group)
- Examination of progress in order to problem solve for greater performance

The center needs to invest in these very conditions that result in greater focus, capacity, and commitment at the level of day-to-day practice. They invest, in other words, in establishing conditions for greater local responsibility. In this process, the center will still want goals, standards, assessment, proof of implementation, and evidence of progress. This means investment in resources and mechanisms of internal accountability that people can use to collaborate within their units and across them.

With strong internal accountability as the context, the external accountability role of the system includes the following:

1. Establishing and promoting professional standards and practices, including performance appraisal, undertaken by professionally respected peers and leaders in teams wherever possible and developing the expertise of teachers and teacher-leaders so that they can undertake these responsibilities. With the robust judgments of respected leaders and peers, then getting rid of teachers and administrators who should not be in the profession will become a transparent collective responsibility.

2. Ongoing monitoring of the performance of the system, including direct intervention with schools and districts in cases of persistent underperformance.

3. Insisting on reciprocal accountability that manages "up" as well as down so that systems are held accountable for providing the resources and supports that are essential in enabling schools and teachers to fulfill expectations (e.g., "failing" schools should not be closed when they have been insufficiently resourced, or individual teachers should be evaluated in the context of whether they have been forced into different grade assignments every year or have experienced constant leadership instability).

4. Adopting and applying indicators of organizational health as a context for individual teacher and leader performance, such as staff retention rates, leadership turnover rates, teacher absenteeism levels, numbers of crisis related incidents, and so on, in addition to outcome indicators of student performance and well-being. These would include measures of social capital in the teaching profession such as extent of collaboration and levels of collegial trust. Outcome measures for students should also, as previously stated, include multiple measures including well-being, students' sense of control over their own destiny (locus of control), levels of engagement in learning, and so forth.

The Perspective of Locals

We have drawn on numerous relatively successful examples in this book. They all established strong degrees of internal accountability (people being self and group responsible) that served them well in the external account-ability arena. Such systems strengthened accountability by increasing focus, connecting dots and otherwise working on coherence, building capacity (so people could perform more efficaciously), being transparent about progress and practices, and engaging the external accountability system.

As districts increase their capacity, they become stronger in the face of ill-advised external accountability demands as the following two extended examples reveal from Laura Schwalm, former superintendent of Garden Grove.

Example One: Garden Grove Handles External Pressure

In the words of Laura Schwalm: Shortly after we completed our audit and instituted a districtwide mandate and system to place students in college prep (a–g) courses, Ed Trust and several other advocacy groups, with sup-port from the California Department of Education (CDE), began "calling out" the low college readiness statistics in large urban districts in Califor-nia. Every large urban district, including Garden Grove, was called out (rightfully so) with one exception of a district in the north, which was held as a model solution due to the fact that they had made the a–g require-ment mandatory for every student and claiming they had eliminated all other courses with absolutely no effect on their graduation rate. Based on this example, the advocacy groups started a very public campaign and got a majority of school boards, including LAUSD, to adopt the poli-cies of this northern district with the pledge that they would achieve 100 percent a–g achievement with no increase in dropout rate within four to five years. When Garden Grove refused to comply (Long Beach did as well), we were more strongly targeted and pressured (the approach we had adopted was to not eliminate all support courses that were not college prep but rather to eliminate a few and to align the rest in a way to provide an "on ramp" to college prep courses while at the same time using indi-vidual student-by-student achievement data, rather than the former prac-tice of "teacher recommendation" for placement in college prep courses) (one of the shameful things our audit revealed, which did not surprise me, was that if you were an Asian student with mean achievement on the California Standards Tests, you had about a 95 percent chance of being "recommended for placement in a-g courses"—conversely, if you were a Latino male with the exact same scores, you had less than 30 percent chance of being recommended for placement in these courses).

As the pressure continued to adopt a policy of mandating an exclusive a–g curriculum, I met with a few of the key advocates and explained that while we shared the same goal of increasing our unacceptably low a–g completion rate, we strongly felt the approach they were suggesting was ill advised. Putting students in a course for which they were absolutely not prepared, based on very objective data, and then expecting them to pass the course with a grade of C or better was unfair to both students and teachers. They kept focusing on the district up north, which led me to point out to them that the data from that district did not support what they were claiming. If their approach was truly working, then their achievement scores, as measured by the state, should be outperforming ours, and in fact, they fell far short of ours, for all subgroups. Additionally, a neighboring district that had adopted the same policy now claimed a 90 percent a–g completion rate, yet 65 percent of their high school students scored below the mean on the state standards test. It clearly pointed out that all was not as it looked on the surface, and while I had no desire to criticize another district's approach, I was not about to follow it. That caused the advocates to pause and finally to leave us alone. Our rate, both in terms of a–g completion and student achievement data by subgroup, continued to climb. Within a few years, we surpassed all the others, and over time, the policy the CDE and advocates had pushed into districts quietly vanished. Unfortunately, in many places where it vanished, a robust and fair system did not replace it, and those districts continue to struggle with this problem (L. Schwalm, personal communication, 2014).

Example Two: Garden Grove Deals With the Bureaucracy

Again in Schwalm's words: Another example occurred during one of the CDE's three-year systemwide compliance reviews. While I accepted the state's responsibility to oversee that we were not using specially designated funding for inappropriate uses, as well as to assure we were following laws around equity and access for all students, the process they had was unnecessarily burdensome, requiring us to dedicate significant staff to collecting, cataloging, and preparing documentation that filled dozens and dozens of boxes. When the state team came—usually about 10 to 12 people, each looking at different programs with one person loosely designated as team lead—the expectation was that you treat them like royalty and that they had enormous authority. My view was somewhat different. I respected that they had a job to do, but just because they did not like the way we displayed something did not mean we needed to do it differently or because they would have used another approach—our approach, if appropriately supported with data—was not out of bounds. At one of the first reviews early on in my superintendency, we drew a particularly weak but officious team with a very weak lead. They came up with some particularly lame findings (i.e., one team member commended us on how we used data to identify areas of focus for targeted groups of students, while another team member marked us as noncompliant in this area because we did not put it on a form that she had developed—and other equally ludicrous examples). At the end of the process, the superintendent was required to sign an agreement validating the team's findings as well as a plan and timeline to bring things into "compliance." I very professionally told them that I did not agree with their findings and thus could not sign either document—I was not going to pretend to fix something that I had no intention of doing because there was nothing wrong with it in the first place. What I did do was sign a document, which we drafted, acknowledging that the team had, in fact, been there and that we agreed to a couple of specific areas where we needed to and would make some changes, but I did not agree with the majority of the report and would not agree to take any action other than what was previously specified. This seemed pretty fair to me, but apparently it shocked them and the system, which was the beginning of my unpopularity with many in CDE. Probably this was made worse when the story got out (not by my telling), and other superintendents realized that they could do the same thing (although I advised those who contacted me—and a number did—that their life would not be particularly easy for awhile and also that they should have the data and results to back their stand) (L. Schwalm, personal communication, 2014).

You can see why in another book (where I cited an even more egregious example of defiance) I referred to Laura as a "rebel with a cause" (Fullan, 2015). There are two lessons here with what I have called both the freedom-from problem and the freedom-to problem. You need to attend to both. The freedom-from problem is what Laura did—refusing to comply with ridiculous demands. But she was backed up by her freedom-to actions in which she built a culture of coherence, capacity, and internal accountability. If you do the latter, you are in good shape to contend with the external accountability system, including acting on external performance data that do show that you need to improve.

In California as a whole, they currently face the freedom-to problem. The wrong drivers are on the way out the door. Jerry Brown, the governor, has suspended all statewide student tests for at least two years on the grounds that it is better to have no tests than to have the wrong test. So far so good, but getting rid of bad tests is not enough for securing accountability. New tests—Smarter Balanced Assessment Curriculum (SBAC)—are being piloted relative to CCSS. Districts would be well advised to use our Coherence Framework to build their focused accountability. They will then perform better and be in a better position to secure their own accountability as they relate to the ups and downs of external accountability. External accountability as wrong as it can get sometimes is a phenomenon that keeps you honest. Leaders need to be skilled at both internal and external accountability and their interrelationship.

Final Thoughts

In sum, local leaders have to play their part in establishing internal accountability and in relating to the external accountability system. The most direct way of understanding what is needed for internal accountability is to work diligently on the first three components of the Coherence Framework: focusing direction, cultivating collaborative cultures, and deepening learning. In many ways, this is tantamount to establishing the conditions for individuals and the group to be accountable to themselves. Part and parcel of internal accountability involves discussing it among staff: what are we trying to do, how well are we progressing, how we define accountability among ourselves, and so on.

In addition, it is essential *to engage* the external policy and accountability system. This does not mean you follow orders; we mentioned earlier about the need to "move unproductive compliance to the side of the plate," and, certainly, Laura exemplifies this quality. But it does mean that you take the state vision seriously; you track your progress relative to state goals and to other schools and districts. A good, basic way to address the outside is to participate in it. This means being part of networks, presenting at regional and state conferences, and contributing to the betterment of the overall system through helping others. It means being plugged into what is happening on the outside.

Securing accountability is not about pleasing the system (although there is nothing wrong with that) but about acting in ways that are in your own interest. In other words, if you address the sequence of internal and external accountability as we have discussed it in this chapter, you will be furthering your own ends. Think of accountability as integral to the Coherence Framework. It is not something you do as an afterthought. If you address accountability explicitly as we have set out in this chapter, you will be strengthening focused vision (to be accountable is to be precise about what you are doing), building better collaboration (because it is for a measurable cause), and deepening learning (because the agenda these days has shifted to 21st century learning goals that have been hitherto neglected).

Throughout the chapters, we have talked about leadership. It is now time to step back and to address it in its own right. What do you need to know and do to lead for coherence? More importantly, how can you cultivate such leadership in others? Effective leaders must help the entire organization cultivate the Coherence Framework in its daily culture.

Review Infographic 5 to consolidate your knowledge about Securing Accountability.

Internal Accountability

Internal accountability is based on the notion that individuals *and* the group in which they work can transparently hold themselves responsible for their performance.

 Successful schools build a collaborative culture that combines individual responsibility, collective expectations, and corrective action.

Internal accountability must precede external accountability if lasting improvement in student achievement is the goal.

Policy makers and other leaders should establish conditions for developing cultures of internal accountability.

Individuals should develop collaborative work with peers and push upward for this work to be supported.

Local leaders have to play their part in establishing internal accountability and in relating to the external accountability system.

 It is essential *to engage* the external policy and accountability sytem.

 Focusing Direction — Cultivating Collaborative Cultures — **Leadership** — Deepening Learning

 Securing Accountability

The best approach for securing accountability is to develop conditions that maximize "internal accountability" and reinforce internal accountability with external accountability.

The Perspective of Locals

Successful systems establish strong degrees of internal accountability that serve them well in the external accountability arena.

 External Accountability

External Authorities

The more that internal accountability thrives, the greater the responsiveness to external requirements and the less the externals have to do.

Central authorities should focus their efforts on two interrelated activities:

1. Investing in internal accountability

2. Projecting and protecting the system

A full-color version of this infographic is also available for download at http://www.corwin.com/books/Book244044 under "About" and then "Sample Materials and Chapters."

6

Leading for Coherence

Our Coherence Framework is "simplexity." Simplexity is not a real word, but it is a valuable concept. Simplexity means that you take a difficult problem and identify a small number of key factors (about four to six)—this is the simple part. And then you make these factors gel under the reality of action with its pressures, politics, and personalities in the situation—this is the complex part. In the case of our framework, there are only four big chunks and their interrelationships. Not only are these components dynamic but also they get refined over time in the setting in which you work. You have to focus on the right things, but you also must learn as you go. One of our favorite insights came from a retired CEO from a very successful company who, when asked about the most important thing he has learned about leadership, responded by saying, "It is more important to be right at the end of the meeting than the beginning" (David Cote, Honeywell, nyti.ms/1chUHqp). He was using this as a metaphor for a good change process: leaders influence the group, but they also learn from it. In fact, joint learning is what happens in effective change processes. If you are right at the beginning of the meeting, you are right only in your own mind. If you are right at the notional end of the meeting, it means that you have processed the ideas with the group.

McKinsey & Company conducted a study of leaders in the social sector (education et al.) and opened their report with these words: "chronic underinvestment [in leadership development] is placing increasing demands on social sector leaders" (Callanan, Gardner, Mendonca, & Scott, 2014). Their conclusions are right in our wheelhouse. In the survey of 200 social sector leaders, participants rated four critical attributes: balancing innovation with implementation, building executive teams, collaborating, and managing outcomes. Survey respondents found themselves and their peers to be deficient in all four domains. In one table, they show the priorities—ability to innovate and implement, ability to surround selves with talented teams, collaboration, and ability to manage to outcomes—in terms of how respondents rated themselves and rated their peers as strong in the given domain. Both sets of scores were low—all below 40 percent. Collaboration, for example, was rated as 24 percent (self-rating) and 24 percent (rating of their peers). So the top capabilities are in short supply.

Leaders build coherence when they combine the four components of our Coherence Framework to meet the varied needs of the complex organizations they lead. Coherence making is a forever job because people come and go, and the situational dynamics are always in flux. They actively develop lateral and vertical connections so that the collaborative culture is deepened and drives deepened learning and reinforces the focused direction.

Achieving coherence in a system takes a long time and requires continuous attention. The main threat to coherence is turnover at the top with new leaders who come in with their own agenda. It is not turnover per se that is the problem, but rather discontinuity of direction. Sometimes systems performing poorly do require a shakeup, but we have also seen situations where new leaders disrupt rather than build on the good things that are happening. And we have seen (more rarely in our experience) districts like Garden Grove where there was a change of superintendents based on a deliberate plan to continue and deepen the effectiveness of the system. The idea in changeover ideally combines continuity *and* innovation. As we have said, coherence making and re-making is a never-ending proposition.

The previous chapters contain many ideas about leadership, and we hope the reader has garnered key lessons in relation to each of the four components of the framework. We won't repeat these ideas here. Instead, we boil down leadership to two big recommendations: master the framework, and develop leaders at all levels.

Master the Framework

Although some degree of linearity is implied in the framework, we intend it to be employed simultaneously. Think holistically as you drill down on each component. Focusing direction and collaborating is a two-way street. As a leader, you should have good ideas about the moral imperative, but these ideas will not be refined until you interact with the group. Collaborating with purpose—the quality change process we talked about—helps to define purpose in practice and builds capacity that results in greater clarity and efficacy. More and more we see the education agenda being immersed with deep learning. This means innovation and continuous improvement coexist—always a difficult proposition.

Figure 6.1 contains our full framework. Like any plan, in addition to its quality and comprehensiveness, it is essential to build a commonly owned approach. The leaders can read our book, and if the ideas seem to have potential, they can begin to discuss the approach with others. They can then begin to form a plan based on the four components of the framework.

Figure 6.1   The Coherence Framework

There are many different ways to proceed. Here are a few: conduct a mental inventory with others by applying the framework to your system to examine whether you have included everything and to determine how well you are doing on each sub-item; discuss the framework among your leadership team, starting with the four main headings to see if the ideas resonate; start discussing the main concepts with other leaders in the system as you begin to form plans and strategies; and start through action forums, working on the four domains.

However you go about it, take the advice we gave in Chapter 2: *participate as a learner* working alongside others to move the organization forward. The framework is not a blueprint but a prompt to assess whether you are actually addressing the four components and the 13 subcomponents. Use the framework to get a 360-degree snapshot of how the coherence is perceived at all levels. To get you started, we provide a Coherence Assessment Tool in Figure 6.2. The tool includes the four components and prompts for starting discussions about the subcomponents. We encourage you to focus on identifying the evidence of each element in your organization. You may want to have individuals in different roles in the organization reflect and then combine those reflections to get a full picture. Consider areas where perceptions are similar and use areas that are different as starting points for deeper conversations—Is your approach comprehensive enough? Are you addressing all four components? Consider your strengths but also the areas of greatest need as you review the four parts of the framework, and identify ways you can leverage the former and develop the latter. There is no one right formula—but what's important is to use the exercise to move to action.

Once again, the strongest change process shapes and reshapes quality ideas as it builds capacity and ownership among participants. As you become stronger and stronger in practicing the Coherence Framework, you will get greater enthusiasm and greater results that will spur people on to accomplish more. "Talking the walk," as we have said, is both a great indicator and a great strategy for the group to become clearer and more committed individually and collectively. Can leaders at all levels clearly describe the framework as it is being used in the system?

Figure 6.2   Coherence Assessment Tool

Component		Evidence
Fostering Direction	Shared purpose drives action.	
	A small number of goals tied to student learning drive decisions.	
	A clear strategy for achieving the goals is known by all.	
	Change knowledge is used to move the school/district/system forward.	
Creating Collaborative Cultures	A growth mind-set underlies the culture.	
	Leaders model learning themselves and shape a culture of learning.	
	Collective capacity building is fostered above individual development.	
	Structures and processes support intentional collaborative work.	

(Continued)

Figure 6.2 (Continued)

Component		Evidence
Deepening Learning	Learning goals are clear to everyone and drive instruction.	
	A set of effective pedagogical practices is known and used by all educators.	
	Robust processes (collaborative inquiry and examining student work) are used regularly to improve practice.	
Securing Accountability	Capacity building is used to continuously improve results.	
	Underperformance is an opportunity for growth, not blame.	
	External accountability is used transparently to benchmark progress.	

As you use the Coherence Framework to reflect on organizational coherence, you can also think of progress in terms of developing specific leadership competencies. Kirtman and Fullan (2015) show how the seven competencies of highly effective leaders mesh with "whole system improvement." The seven skills are listed in Figure 6.3.

Figure 6.3 Leadership Competencies for Whole System Improvement

1. Challenges the status quo	5. Has a high sense of urgency for change and sustainable results
2. Builds trust through clear communications and expectations	6. Commits to continuous improvement
3. Creates a commonly owned plan for success	7. Builds external networks/partnerships
4. Focuses on team over self	

These competencies map on our Coherence Framework. Challenging the status quo is part and parcel of focusing new directions. Building trust and creating a commonly owned plan are very much part of collaborating with purpose. Focusing on the team is about leadership development in others. The next two—sense of urgency in relation to results and continuous improvement—relate directly to internal and external accountability. External networks and partnerships is a wraparound set of collaborative activities that enable leaders to both use and contribute to the external environment.

Most leaders, as the McKinsey & Company's study revealed, are not good at leading the change process. Mastering our framework will address that deficit and enable you and your system to become much more effective and much more likely to become more sustainable.

And you don't have to do it alone; indeed, it cannot be done alone. It takes the group to change the group, and it takes many leaders to change the group. This is why developing leaders at all levels is essential.

••
Develop Leaders at All Levels
••

One of the strongest factors that contributed to the success of Ontario's systemwide growth involved the development of leaders at all levels—school, district, and government. One of the marks of an effective leader is not only the impact that they have on the bottom line of student achievement but also equally how many good leaders they leave behind. Thus, effective leaders choose, mentor, and otherwise develop other leaders. This has two payoffs. In the short run, there is more impact because of a critical mass of leaders who are working in a focused way on the same agenda. In the long term, the impact is even more powerful because these leaders form a critical mass of leaders for the next phase. To put it one way, junior members of a learning organization are being groomed for the future, as they get better in the present. One way of putting it oddly is to say that effective leaders develop teams of leaders and, consequently, if they are successful, become more *dispensable* to their organizations because they have developed a cadre of other leaders who can carry on and go deeper. Whereas if the individual leader is dominant, they leave a vacuum when they depart. Even if they are successful, their impact is superficial because too much depends on them as individuals. The goal is to make yourself dispensable as a leader so you and your organization can go on to further progress.

You should invest in leadership development in others in informal and formal ways. First, collaborative cultures develop leadership naturally within the ongoing culture. Such cultures are learning cultures and, consequentially, are always working on the development of leaders, day-after-day built into the culture itself. In addition to the informal culture, it is necessary to invest in more organized or formal leadership development. The McKinsey & Company report says that "effective CEOs surround themselves with people possessing the diverse skills that a successful organization needs. Social sector leaders seem to recognize this and prioritize it, but their responses suggest that they have not been successful" (p. 3). So, the first order of business is for education leaders to recognize that one of their key roles is to develop the leadership of others—to develop the active bench strength of existing leaders in the organization.

Primarily, this is a normative job. By that, we mean that the leader should establish a learning culture in which many people are expected to develop their leadership skills and help others do the same. Leaders developing other leaders becomes the natural order of the day. In addition, the organization should develop and use other tools to systematically foster leadership in the system. This would include mentoring, coaching, giving feedback, interning, and training in key skills such as communication and media skills. In our model, the difference is that these more formal strategies do not serve as *drivers* but as reinforcers of the direction of the organization generated by our four-part Coherence Framework.

Again, Ontario did this well. Regular business concentrated on focused direction, collaboration, increasingly deeper learning, and internal accountability—all to serve the three core goals: increase student achievement, reduce the gap, and increase the public confidence in the public school system (latterly, Ontario has added a fourth goal: the well-being of students). To back this up, the leadership unit within the ministry developed (in partnership with districts) tools—leadership frameworks and strategies—to cultivate leadership within districts and schools (www .education-leadership-ontario.ca). There are two crucial elements of this strategy. One is that formal leadership development was expressly in the service of implementing the main agenda of the three core goals. They reinforced and were in the same direction as the core agenda. The leadership strategy was a supporter and reinforcer, not a driver. Second—and this is remarkable—the leadership framework tool was never compulsory, *but everyone uses it.* It became commonly owned because the process drew people to the best solution that has now become a requirement (every district must develop a leadership succession plan). The end result is that the day-to-day evolution of activities akin to the Coherence Framework is reinforced by actions that foster ongoing leadership development tools.

Review Infographic 6, on page 138, to clarify how you will use leadership to integrate the four components of the Coherence Framework.

Final Thoughts

There has never been a more important time to be your own leader. In terms of the right drivers in action, we are seeing small signs that some policy makers are realizing that using the wrong drivers of punitive accountability, focusing on individuals, purchasing technology, and jumping from one ad hoc policy to another is no way to achieve coherence. Right now, there is a vacuum of direction. Vacuums can be filled with fruitless and wrong ideas. Or they can be filled with focused direction, purposeful collaboration, deep learning, and self and other accountability. Leaders in the social sector have a special responsibility to pursue through education the moral imperative of societal development: balance innovation and continuous improvement, build teams with focus and efficacy, and manage toward deep outcomes.

The Coherence Framework, and especially its focus on deepening learning outcomes, is crucial at this particular juncture in history. By and large, society and prospects for students in the present and projected future have been declining since the 1970s. This decline—fewer and fewer jobs, the dramatically growing financial gap between the narrowing top and the expanding bottom—is accelerating with no relief and no solutions evident. Brynjolfsson and McAfee's *The Second Machine Age* (2014) and Ford's *Rise of Robots: Technology and the Threat of a Jobless Future* (2015) document with strong evidence and paint these threatening scenarios in vivid terms (still, not a simple matter; see McKinsey & Company's *A Labor Market That Works: Connecting Talent With Opportunity in the Digital Age* [2015]). In any case, the education system, and society at large, have been sluggish to respond and are now faced with a race for survival, the likes of which we have never experienced. Put another way, we are not talking about mere coherence of existing elements, but a radical transformation into deep learning with all of its associated parts. This is the coherence challenge!

Here is a reminder that the audience for this book—those who have to take action—are leaders at all levels of the education system. Local school and district leaders (including parent and community leaders) must set their sights on mobilizing for coherence. In addition to internal development of their schools, they must also link to the wider political and policy arena by proactively engaging in state priorities and policies, sometimes blunting directives that are distracting but mostly by figuring out how to use external requirements to improve local performance. Politicians and other policy makers must make a decided shift away from relying on wrong drivers toward making the right drivers the center of gravity for action and assessment. Each group must do its own part with an eye to partnerships and coalescing of energies. The result will be greater and sustainable whole system performance.

It is time to take action in order to find and link to the kindred spirits that are willing to join you on this critical journey. Take the actions we have outlined, and be the catalyst that makes it easy for you to find and for you to be found by the critical mass that could make a lasting difference. Others are waiting to join. Be the connector who activates them. Connect locally, regionally, and beyond. Make a difference by being a coherence maker in chaotic times!

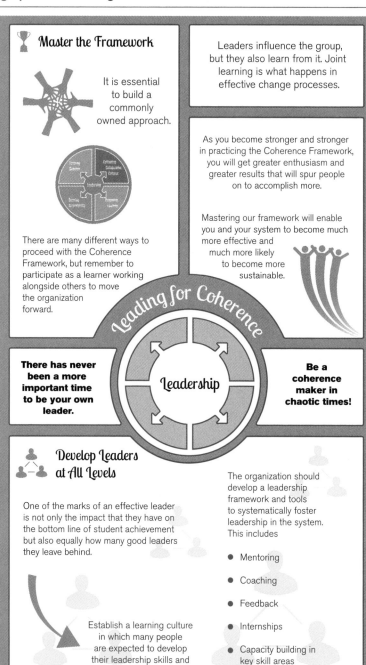

🏆 **Master the Framework**

It is essential to build a commonly owned approach.

Leaders influence the group, but they also learn from it. Joint learning is what happens in effective change processes.

As you become stronger and stronger in practicing the Coherence Framework, you will get greater enthusiasm and greater results that will spur people on to accomplish more.

There are many different ways to proceed with the Coherence Framework, but remember to participate as a learner working alongside others to move the organization forward.

Mastering our framework will enable you and your system to become much more effective and much more likely to become more sustainable.

Leading for Coherence

Leadership

There has never been a more important time to be your own leader.

Be a coherence maker in chaotic times!

👥 **Develop Leaders at All Levels**

One of the marks of an effective leader is not only the impact that they have on the bottom line of student achievement but also equally how many good leaders they leave behind.

The organization should develop a leadership framework and tools to systematically foster leadership in the system. This includes

- Mentoring
- Coaching
- Feedback
- Internships
- Capacity building in key skill areas

Establish a learning culture in which many people are expected to develop their leadership skills and help others do the same.

A full-color version of this infographic is also available for download at **http://www.corwin.com/books/Book244044** under "About" and then "Sample Materials and Chapters."

References and Further Readings

Barber, M., & Mourshed, M. (2007). *How the world's best-performing school systems come out on top.* London, UK: McKinsey & Company.

The Boston Consulting Group. (2014). *Teachers know best: Teachers' views on professional development.* Washington, DC: Bill and Melinda Gates Foundation.

Brown, T. (2015). *Big idea 2015: The unexpected path to creative breakthroughs.* Retrieved from www.designthinking.ideo.com

Bryk, A., Bender Sebring, P. B., Allensworth, E., Luppescu, S., & Easton, J. Q. (2010). *Organizing schools for improvement: Lessons from Chicago.* Chicago, IL: University of Chicago Press.

Bryk, A., Gomez, L., Grunow, A., & Le Mahieu, P. (2014). *Learning to improve: How America's schools can get better at getting better.* Cambridge, MA: Harvard Education Press.

Brynjolfsson, E., & McAfee, A. (2014). *The second machine age.* New York: Norton.

Callanan, L., Gardner, N., Mendonca, L., & Scott, D. (2014, November). What social-sector leaders need to succeed. *Insights & Publications.* London, UK: McKinsey & Company.

City, E., Elmore, R., Fiarman, S., & Teitel, L. (2009). *Instructional rounds in education: A network approach to improving teaching and learning.* Cambridge, MA: Harvard Education Press.

Csikszentmihalyi, M. (2008). *Flow: The psychology of optimal experience.* New York, NY: HarperCollins.

Cuban, L. (2014). *Inside the black box of classroom practice: Change without reform in American education.* Cambridge, MA: Harvard University Press.

DuFour, R., & Eaker, R. (1998). *Professional learning communities at work: Best practices for enhancing student achievement.* Bloomington, IN: Solution Tree.

DuFour, R., & Fullan, M. (2013). *Built to last: Systemic PLCs at work.* Bloomington, IN: Solution Tree.

Edutopia. (n.d.). *Lessons from a public school turnaround: Cochrane Collegiate Academy.* Retrieved from http://www.edutopia.org/stw-school-turnaround

Edwards, M. (2015). *Thank you for your leadership.* Hoboken, NJ: Pearson Education.

Eells, R. (2011). *Meta analysis of the relationship between collective efficacy and student achievement.* Dissertation, Loyola University, Chicago, UMI No. 2469968.

Elmore, R. (2004). *School reform from the inside out: Policy, practice, and performance.* Cambridge, MA: Harvard University Press.

Ford, M. (2015). *Rise of robots: Technology and the threat of a jobless future.* New York, NY: Basic Books.

Fullan, M. (2010). *All systems go: The change imperative for whole school reform.* Thousand Oaks, CA: Corwin.

Fullan, M. (2011a). Choosing the wrong drivers for whole system reform. *Seminar Series 204.* Melbourne, Australia: Center for Strategic Education.

Fullan, M. (2011b). *The moral imperative realized.* Thousand Oaks, CA: Corwin.

Fullan, M. (2013a). *Great to excellent: Launching the next stage of Ontario's education agenda.* Retrieved from www.edu.gov.on.ca/eng/document/reports/FullanReport_EN_07.pdf

Fullan, M. (2013b). The new pedagogy: Students and teachers as learning partners. *LEARNing Landscapes, 6*(2), 23–28.

Fullan, M. (2013c). *Stratosphere: Integrating technology, pedagogy, and change knowledge.* Toronto, Canada: Pearson.

Fullan, M. (2014a). *California's golden opportunity: A status note.* Retrieved from www.michaelfullan.ca

Fullan, M. (2014b). *Motion leadership film series.* Retrieved from www.michael fullan.ca

Fullan, M. (2014c). *The principal: Three keys for maximizing impact.* San Francisco, CA: Jossey-Bass.

Fullan, M. (2015). *Freedom to change: Four strategies to put your inner drive into overdrive.* San Francisco, CA: Jossey-Bass.

Fullan, M. (in press). *The new meaning of educational change* (5th ed.). New York, NY: Teachers College Press.

Fullan, M., & Boyle, A. (2014). *Big-city school reforms: Lessons from New York, Toronto, and London.* New York, NY: Teachers College Press.

Fullan, M., & Rincón-Gallardo, S. (in press). Developing high quality public education in Canada: The case of Ontario. In F. Adamson, B. Astrand, & L. Darling-Hammond (Eds.), *Global education reform: Privatization vs. public investments in national education systems.* New York, NY: Routledge.

Fullan, M., Rincón-Gallardo, S., & Hargreaves, A. (2015). Professional capital as accountability. *Education Policy Analysis Archives, 23*(15), 1–18.

Fullan, M., & Scott, G. (2014). *Education plus.* Seattle, WA: Collaborative Impact.

Gallagher, M. J. (2014). *Ontario education improvement. Slide deck for international presentations.* Toronto, Canada: Ministry of Education.

Gallup Poll. (2014). *Gallup student poll: Measuring student hope, engagement and well-being.* Washington, DC: Author.

Glaze, A. E., Mattingley, R. E., & Andrews, R. (2013). *High school graduation: K–12 strategies that work.* Thousand Oaks, CA: Corwin.

Hadfield, C. (2014). *You are here: Around the world in 92 minutes: Photographs from the International Space Station.* Toronto, Canada: Random House.

Hargreaves, A., & Braun, H. (2012). *Leading for all: A research report of the development, design, implementation and impact of Ontario's "Essential for Some, Good for All" initiative.* Boston, MA: Boston College.

Hargreaves, A., Boyle, A., & Harris, A. (2014). *Uplifting leadership: How organizations, teams and communities raise performance.* San Francisco, CA: Jossey-Bass.

Hargreaves, A., & Fullan, M. (2012). *Professional capital: Transforming teaching in every school.* New York, NY: Teachers College Press.

Hargreaves, A., & Shirley, D. (2009). *The fourth way: The inspiring future for educational change.* Thousand Oaks, CA: Corwin.

Hattie, J. (2009). *Visible learning: A synthesis of over 800 meta-analyses relating to achievement.* New York, NY: Routledge.

Hattie, J. (2012). *Visible learning for teachers.* New York, NY: Routledge.

Hattie, J. (2015). *What works best in education: The politics of collaborative expertise.* London, UK: Pearson.

Herman, J. (2013). *Canada's approach to school funding: The adoption of provincial control of education funding in three provinces.* Washington, DC: Center for American Progress. Retrieved from http://www.americanprogress.org/wp-content/uploads/2013/05/HermanCanadaReport.pdf

Hill, M. L. (Host). (2015, April 8). *Atlanta teachers face 20 years in cheating scandal* [Video podcast]. Retrieved from live.huffingtonpost.com/r/segment/551ee2962b8c2afbd6000392

Huffington, A. (2014). *Thrive: The third metric to redefining success and creating a life of well-being, wisdom and wonder.* New York, NY: Harmony Books.

Jenkins, L. (2013). *Permission to forget.* Milwaukee, WI: American Society for Quality Press.

Johnson, S. M. (2004). *Finders and keepers: Helping new teachers thrive and survive in our schools.* San Francisco, CA: Jossey-Bass.

Johnson, S. M., Marietta, G., Higgins, M., Mapp, K., & Grossman, A. (2015). *Achieving coherence in district improvement.* Cambridge, MA: Harvard Education Press.

Joyce, B., & Calhoun, E. (2010). *Models of professional development: A celebration of educators.* Thousand Oaks, CA: Corwin.

Kirtman, L. (2013). *Leadership and teams: The missing piece of the education reform puzzle.* Upper Saddle River, NJ: Pearson Education.

Kirtman, L., & Fullan, M. (2015). *Leadership: Key competencies for whole-system change.* Bloomington, IN: Solution Tree.

Kluger, J. (2008). *Simplexity.* New York, NY: Hyperion Books.

Knudson, J. (2013). *You'll never be better than your teachers: The Garden Grove approach to human capital improvement, California Collaborative on District Reform.* Washington, DC: American Institutes for Research.

Leana, C. (2011). The missing link in school reform. *Stanford School Innovation Review, 9*(4), 30–35.

Leskiw-Janvary, K., Oakes, L., & Waler, C. (2013). Principal learning teams in the District School Board of Niagara. *OPC Register, 15*(2).

Marzano, R. (2003). *What works in schools: Translating research into action.* Alexandria, VA: Association for Supervision and Curriculum Development.

McKinsey & Company. (2015). *A labor market that works: Connecting talent with opportunity in the digital age.* McKinsey Global Institute.

Mehta, J., Schwartz, R. B., & Hess, F. M. (2012). *The futures of school reform*. Cambridge, MA: Harvard Education Press.

Michael Fullan Enterprises & California Forward. (2015). *Golden opportunity: The California collaborative for education excellence as a force for positive change*. Authors.

Mourshed, M., Chijioke, C., & Barber, M. (2010). *How the world's most improved school systems keep getting better.* London, UK: McKinsey & Company.

New Hampshire Department of Education. (2013, Summer). *The New Hampshire Network Strategy.* Concord, NH: Department of Education.

New Pedagogies for Deep Learning (NPDL). (2014). Retrieved from www .NPDL.global

November, A. (2012). *Who owns the learning?* Bloomington, IN: Solution Tree.

Ontario Ministry of Education. (2007a). *Ontario focused intervention partnership*. Toronto, Canada: Queen's Printer for Ontario. Retrieved from http://www .edu.gov.on.ca/eng/literacynumeracy/ofip.html

Ontario Ministry of Education. (2007b). Teacher moderation: Collaborative assessment of student work. *Capacity Building Series*. Retrieved from http://www .edu.gov.on.ca/eng/literacynumeracy/inspire/research/capacityBuilding.html

Ontario Ministry of Education. (2009). *Schools on the move (Lighthouse Program)*. Toronto, Canada: Queen's Printer for Ontario. Retrieved from http://www .edu.gov.on.ca/eng/literacynumeracy/onthemove.pdf

Ontario Ministry of Education. (2012). *Ontario leadership strategy and framework*. Retrieved from http://www.edu.gov.on.ca/eng/policyfunding/ leadership/framework.html

Ontario Ministry of Education. (2014). *Achieving excellence: A renewed vision for education in Ontario*. Toronto, Canada: Ministry of Education. Retrieved from http://www.edu.gov.on.ca/eng/about/renewedVision.pdf

Organisation for Economic Cooperation and Development. (2011). Ontario, Canada: Reform to support high achievement in a diverse context. In *Strong performers and successful reformers in education: Lessons from PISA for the United States*. Retrieved from http://www.oecd.org/pisa/pisaproducts/46580959.pdf

Organisation for Economic Cooperation and Development. (2013). *Teachers for the 21st century: Using evaluation to improve teaching*. Paris, France: Author.

Park, S., & Takahashi, S. (2013). *90-day cycle handbook*. Stanford, CA: Carnegie Foundation for the Advancement of Teaching.

Pil, F., & Leana, C. (2006). Applying organizational research in public school reform. *Academy of Management Journal, 52*(6), 1101–1124.

Pink, D. (2009). *Drive: The surprising truth about what motivates us*. New York, NY: Penguin Books.

Quaglia, R., & Corso, M. (2014). *Student voice: The instrument of change*. Thousand Oaks, CA: Corwin.

Ries, E. (2011). *The lean startup: How today's entrepreneurs use continuous innovation to create radically successful businesses*. New York, NY: Crown Publishing.

Robinson, V., Lloyd, C., & Rowe, K. (2008). The impact of leadership on student outcomes. *Education Administration Quarterly, 44,* 635–674.

Sattler, P. (2012). Education governance reform in Ontario: Neoliberalism in context. *Canadian Journal of Educational Administration and Policy, 128.*

Schmidt, E., & Cohen, J. (2013). *The new digital age: Reshaping the future of people, nations and business.* New York, NY: Knopf.

Sunstein, C., & Hastie, R. (2014). *Wiser: Getting beyond groupthink to make groups smarter.* Boston, MA: Harvard Business Review Press.

Timperley, H. (2011). *Realizing the power of professional learning.* London, UK: McGraw-Hill.

Tucker, M. (2011). *Standing on the shoulders of giants: An American agenda for education reform.* Washington, DC: National Center on Education and the Economy.

Zavadsky, H. (2009). *Bringing school reform to scale: Five award-winning urban districts.* Cambridge, MA: Harvard Education Press.

Index

Acknowledgments

We are engaged in exciting change projects around the world and privileged to learn from effective leaders who are taking their organizations on the journey toward coherence. This book is the product of many influences, and we are indebted to the growing community who willingly share their journeys toward coherence, including all the Ontario educators; the Idaho Leads team; and the California crowd, including a host of leaders at all levels of the state, from schools and districts to nonprofit organizations, professional associations, including unions, administrator and school board associations, the state superintendent, and the governor. And our thanks go to the many countries around the world with whom we are working on the coherence agenda. Thanks especially to the Stuart Foundation who supports much of our work in California.

First, we are deeply grateful to colleagues with whom we began the journey to crystallize the ideas of whole system change in the field: Eleanor Adam, Al Bertani, Gayle Gregory, Bill Hogarth, Carol Rolheiser, and Nancy Watson. As well, our thanks go to the world of colleagues and thought leaders who challenge and deepen the thinking: Kathleen Budge, the late Greg Butler, Davis Campbell, MaryJean Gallagher, Andy Hargreaves, Lisa Kinnamon, Ken Leithwood, John Malloy, Gabriella Mafi, Joanne McEachen, Bill Parrett, Christy Pitchel, and Laura Schwalm. Next, we wish to thank our global partners in the New Pedagogies for Deep Learning: A Global Partnership (NPDL) who contribute to the evolution of our thinking as they create a social movement to transform learning in Australia, Canada, Finland, Netherlands, New Zealand, United States, and Uruguay. A special acknowledgment goes to Eleanor Adam for her insights and contribution to the concepts, her valuable feedback on the manuscript, and to being a key capacity builder on our team.

This book would not be possible without our professional support team: Claudia Cuttress, who guides the infrastructure and attended to the coherence of the book; to Taryn Hauritz for her inspired infographic summaries that capture the essence of the concepts; and to Arnis Burvikovs, Melanie Birdsall, Megan Markanich, and the rest of the great publishing team at Corwin who combine quality with innovation.

Finally, thank you to our families who provide the support and inspiration in all of our endeavors.

There are many Irish expressions we like, and one of our favorites is "if you are not confused, you probably don't understand the situation." In this book, we hope we have contributed to a degree of growing coherence on your part for the critical societal agenda before us. This book is dedicated to all the coherence makers who inspired this work and the leaders who will guide the future. It's time to make a difference!

About the Authors

Michael Fullan, Order of Canada, is professor emeritus at the Ontario Institute for Studies in Education, University of Toronto. He served as special adviser in education to former premier of Ontario Dalton McGuinty from 2003 to 2013 and now serves as one of four advisers to Premier Kathleen Wynne. Michael has been awarded honorary doctorates from the University of Edinburgh, University of Leicester, Nipissing University, Duquesne University, and the Hong Kong Institute of Education. He consults with governments and school systems in several countries.

Fullan has won numerous awards for his more than 30 books, including the 2015 Grawemeyer Award in Education with Andy Hargreaves for *Professional Capital.* His books include the best sellers *Leading in a Culture of Change, The Six Secrets of Change, Change Leader, All Systems Go, Motion Leadership,* and *The Principal: Three Keys to Maximizing Impact.* His latest books are *Evaluating and Assessing Tools in the Digital Swamp* (with Katelyn Donnelly), *Leadership: Key Competencies for Whole-System Change* (with Lyle Kirtman), *The New Meaning of Educational Change* (5th edition), and *Freedom to Change.* To learn more, visit his website at www.michaelfullan.ca.

Joanne Quinn is the director of whole system change and capacity building at Michael Fullan Enterprises, where she leads the design of strategic whole system capacity building at the global, national, and district levels. She also serves as the director of global capacity building for New Pedagogies for Deep Learning: A Global Partnership (NPDL), focused on transforming learning. Previously, she provided leadership at all levels of education as a superintendent, implementation adviser to the Ontario Ministry of Education, director of continuing education at the University of Toronto, and special adviser on international projects. She consults internationally on whole system change, capacity building, leadership, and professional learning and is sought by professional organizations and institutions as a consultant, adviser, and speaker. These diverse leadership roles and her passion to improve learning for all give her a unique perspective on influencing positive change.

A SAGE Company

Helping educators make the greatest impact

CORWIN HAS ONE MISSION: to enhance education through intentional professional learning.

We build long-term relationships with our authors, educators, clients, and associations who partner with us to develop and continuously improve the best evidence-based practices that establish and support lifelong learning.

ONTARIO
PRINCIPALS'
COUNCIL
Exemplary Leadership in Public Education

The Ontario Principals' Council (OPC) is a voluntary association for principals and vice-principals in Ontario's public school system. We believe that exemplary leadership results in outstanding schools and improved student achievement. To this end, we foster quality leadership through world-class professional services and supports. As an ISO 9001 registered organization, we are committed to **"quality leadership—our principal product."**

Solutions you want. Experts you trust. Results you need.

Author Consulting

Author Consulting

On-site professional learning with sustainable results! Let us help you design a professional learning plan to meet the unique needs of your school or district. www.corwin.com/pd

Institutes

Institutes

Corwin Institutes provide collaborative learning experiences that equip your team with tools and action plans ready for immediate implementation. www.corwin.com/institutes

eCourses

eCourses

Practical, flexible online professional learning designed to let you go at your own pace. www.corwin.com/ecourses

Read2Earn

Read2Earn

Did you know you can earn graduate credit for reading this book? Find out how: www.corwin.com/read2earn

Contact an account manager at (800) 831-6640 or visit **www.corwin.com** for more information.